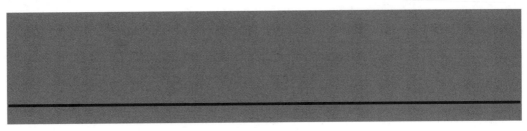

Building Team Spirit

Building Team Spirit

Activities for Inspiring and Energizing Teams

Barry Heermann, Ph.D.

McGraw-Hill

New York   San Francisco   Washington, D.C.   Auckland   Bogotá
Caracas   Lisbon   London   Madrid   Mexico City   Milan
Montreal   New Delhi   San Juan   Singapore
Sydney   Tokyo   Toronto

McGraw-Hill

A Division of The McGraw-Hill Companies

1 2 3 4 5 6 7 8 9 0   EDW/EDW   9 0 2 1 0 9 8 7

ISBN 0-07-028473-3 (paper)
ISBN 0-07-028472-5 (looseleaf)
ISBN 0-07-913618-4

The sponsoring editor for this book was Richard Narramore, the editing supervisor was Fred Dahl, and the production supervisor was Tina Cameron. It was set in Fairfield by Inkwell Publishing Services.

Printed and bound by Edwards Brothers.

Contents

Acknowledgments

The week of May 8, 1993 was the start of it. The magical little community of Tiburon, California, served as the site of a seminar I co-led for Union Institute Ph.D. learners studying organization behavior and/or organization development. I wear several hats, one as an organizational development practitioner, another as a faculty member for the Union Institute. Once each year I am responsible for leading a five-day seminar for Union learners, and in 1993 that was the Tiburon seminar.

My co-leader was a Union learner, Alexandra Kovats. Alexandra is a Dominican nun who worked with Matthew Fox. Fox's eclectic approach to spirit in all of life would become an important subtext for my work in the area of team spirit. I proposed to Alexandra that we collaborate to do this seminar. I would bring my experience as an organization development consultant and my familiarity with a leading team development process (the Team Performance System, developed by Allan Drexler). Alexandra would bring her spiritual awareness and facilitation gifts from her work and affiliation with Matthew Fox. Together we would create something special: a seminar on team spirit.

Little did I know that the seminar would be such a transforming event. I had not considered how I might unite formerly separate worlds, and I was thrilled with the idea. I have always thought spirit was present in my work with groups. A mentor friend of mine in Vermont, Tony Stone, had suggested I am a "spiritual sneak." I like that idea. But something profound happened to me in Tiburon. The wonderful insight and perspective of the 18 learners, many of whom were practitioners and scholars of organization behavior, opened me to a totally new possibility—team spirit.

This book is dedicated to those Union Institute learners and to Alexandra. It is dedicated to my understanding family and my brilliant team leader and wife, Kipra. It is also dedicated to the nearly 200 certified Consultant/Facilitators of Team Spirit, and to the Consultant/Facilitators and organization clients who show up for regular meetings of the Friends of Team Spirit to discuss experiences and approaches at the intersection of spirit and team development.

I wish to acknowledge Gerald Pavloff who has generously provided me consulting support on how to bring Team Spirit to the world; Richard Smith of the Greeleaf Center for Servant Leadership for his always seminal thinking about appropriate metaphors to express my work with spirit in organizations; Stan Sword, Coach of the AT&T GIS (now NCR) Professional Services Organization Development Team, who used Team Spirit to brilliantly develop a high-performing organization and who is now fostering the use of Team Spirit at AT&T Solutions as Resource Director, Outsourcing Practice; and to the following persons for their contribution to particular activities used in this volume: Barbara Czestochowa for the Molding Clay: Letting-Go Metaphor activity and the Meeting Your Inner Servant guided visualization; Skipper Young for the Spirit Walk activity; and Linda Tobey for the Keys to the Kingdom activity. I wish also to acknowledge my good friends Murray Cohen, Bob Ross, Gordon Cowperthwaite, Karen and Roger Fortman, and Peter and Rosemary Jones who always call me to my best in my life and in my relationship with my wife and family. (Karen, Peter, and Rosemary are also Team Spirit Facilitator/Consultants.)

Thanks also to Alyse McConnell, John Waterhouse, Jim Stuart, Diane and Roy Moody, George Barclay, Mary Jo Wetterich, Joe Payne, Peggy Egan, David Schoeff, John Hogan, Basil Zabek, Mary Fay Boyer, Karen Grove, Jonathan Brown, Dick Genardi, Gayle Gyure, Susan Harrington, Skipper Young, Teri and Bill Garcia, Rich Glenn, Rod Goelz, Murray Cohen, Mitch Coleman, Nancy White, Tom Cox, Larry Fidelius, Roger Bourdon, Alex Patakkos, Robert Hernandez, James Ray, Merril Anderson, Sharon Trekell, Katie Buckley, Joe Lawrence, Stacy Fahlsung, Tamara Stuchlak, Cindy Manis, Diane Edelman, Susan Edwards, Nancy Conway, Wendy Appel, Mike Gunther, Julie Raskin, Joleen Jackson, Steve Houchin, Joan Bicocchi, Tammy McNew, Milan Savan, Bob Sweiterman, Karen Ash, Rachel Holstine, Bruce Bertell, Marilyn Spiegel, Jeff Imber, Marcella Balin, Elizabeth David, Joan Cook, Karen Witt, Hardy Hassenfuss, Tanya King, Cheryl Lossie, Carol Rossi, Darlene Weener, Teri Cassady, Chuck Mallue, Luis Marrero, David Mercier, Celine O'Neil, Nancy Henson, Joe Lambright, Fred Schu, Richard Smith, Larry Spears, John Renesch, Linda Garrett, Ted Baxendale, Linda Tobey, Karin Cadwell, Dianna Crowell, Hank Lindborg, Karen Mousain, George O'Brien, Katie Pynn, Angela Smith, Maribeth Quinn, Stu Cart, and Barry Ballard, the latter for editorial support. Thanks, too, to my editor, Richard Narramore, and my publicist, Kathryn Hall, for their wonderful support.

I am especially grateful, and wish to dedicate this book, to my associate Barbara Czestochowa, who has worked tirelessly in the creation of this volume, and to Fred Bartenstein who has so generously given himself to the review of this manuscript and other manuscripts that I have written about Team Spirit. Blessings to all of you.

Barry Heermann

Introduction

...issues of the heart and spirit matter to each of us.
They matter in our families, in our work, and in our extracurricular activities.
We are emotional creatures, trying through the vehicles
of product and knowledge and information and relationships to have an effect for
good on one another both personally
and through what we can do to improve the environment.
Max DePree

This book provides practical activities and interventions that promote team spirit. All of the learning activities in this volume have been used as part of a comprehensive team development program, called Team Spirit, to enhance the spirit of teams and organizations in Fortune 500 companies, major not-for-profits, and small and medium enterprises.

The activities help teams understand and strengthen the relationship of spirit to team and organization performance explored in recent books such as Peter Block's *Stewardship*; Tom Chappell's *Soul of a Business*; Jack Hawley's *Reawakening the Spirit of Work*; David Whyte's *The Heart Aroused*; Margaret Wheatley's *Leadership and the New Science* and *A Simpler Way*; Jay Conger's *Spirit at Work*; Dick Richard's *Artful Work*; and John Renesch's *Rediscovering the Soul of Business* and *The New Bottom Line: Bringing Heart and Soul to Business*.

The learning activities and interventions offered in this book are designed for use by team leaders, organization development facilitators, human resource development facilitators, trainers, and consultants who are seeking practical approaches to nurturing high-performing teams. The outcome is a deeper level of team development that transcends individual differences and leads to brilliant service to customers.

Two introductory chapters provide background and perspective on spirited, high performing teams; the following six chapters contain learning activities and interventions for fostering team spirit. Chapter 1 examines the forces that inhibit the spirit in teams and argues that spirit is the transforming power at the core of all team activity, establishing the relationship of team spirit to team effectiveness. Research on excellence and peak performance confirms that high-performing teams and organizations consistently feel the spirit of the organization in their work, and that this feeling is an essential part of the meaning and value that members and observers place on their work (Vaill, 1989). Chapter 1 names qualities of spirit, portraying them graphically as the Team Spirit Spiral. Chapter 2 suggests the relationship of storytelling to achieving team spirit, and presents stories of teams that exemplify each of the phases of the Spiral.

Chapters 3 through 8 are the heart of the book, with instructions for leading dozens of activities that facilitate the development of spirited teams. Many of the activities provide a platform for teams to tell their stories. The activities in each of these chapters explore the six qualities of spirit that make up the Team Spirit Spiral described in Chapters 1 and 2.

Appendices A and B describe how to use a data gathering tool included in the book, called the Team Spirit Assessment. Appendix C provides lecturettes that can be used in conjunction with several of the learning activities. Appendix D consists of a series of learning activities designed to teach teams the six phases of the Team Spirit Spiral. Appendix E explores the importance of facilitators' nurturing their own spirits and provides learning activities that support and develop the spirit of the facilitator.

FACILITATING THE LEARNING ACTIVITIES

The learning activities in this volume are designed to build the qualities of team spirit discussed in Chapters 1 and 2 and reflected in the Team Spirit Spiral. Becoming a spirited, high-performing team depends upon a variety of factors that are addressed in this book. It is the responsibility of the facilitator to heighten the team's awareness, often by having the team tell their story, and to develop skills that support team members in the process of becoming a spirited, high-performing team.

All the learning activities in this volume include learning goals, necessary preparations (room setup, materials, etc.), easy-to-follow steps for facilitating the learning activity (including timelines and reflections on what can be expected in facilitating the activity), and forms and supporting materials to be used in the presentations or handed out. Occasionally lecturettes are suggested; these are drawn from information provided in Chapters 1 and 2, the introductions to Chapters 3 through 8, and Appendix C.

David Kolb's experiential learning cycle (1984) provides the theoretical learning model that systematically moves participants from concrete experience and reflective observation to abstract conceptualization. Team participants are routinely asked to reflect on the implications of their learning, to record their reactions, and to discuss the experience as part of a culminating group process.

HOW TO USE TEAM SPIRIT ACTIVITIES WITH DIFFERENT TEAM TYPES

The learning activities in this volume are designed for use with "intact teams," that is, existing teams and work groups within an organization. There are three broad categories of intact teams, the first two being defined by their stage of maturity (start-up teams and mature teams) and a third type that is short-term by definition (task forces). A distinct form of team that cuts across these three basic categories is the cross-functional team, which is a team composed of persons who represent different functions and levels of the organization. In organizations that employ this form of team, employees may serve on several cross-functional teams for various durations and for various percentages of their time.

Start-up teams typically require work on the Initiating, Visioning, and Claiming phases of the Team Spirit Spiral during the first six to nine months, followed by work on the Celebrating, Letting Go, and Service phases later in their development.

Mature teams have needs that are reflections of their histories. Their movement through the Team Spirit Spiral is unique to their pattern of conflicts and harmony. Interviews with representative members of the mature team are recommended prior to the development of a program of learning activities. (See Appendices A and B.)

Task forces are formed to accomplish particular short-term outcomes and will disband after fulfilling those outcomes. Task forces are often organized as cross-functional teams, and because of their short duration and the diversity of team membership, these teams must build momentum quickly. Consequently Team Spirit activities can be particularly helpful to this type of fast-paced team, allowing the team to quickly and powerfully develop relationship and vision and take ownership of their work.

APPLICATIONS OF TEAM SPIRIT

Some readers of this volume will use *Building Team Spirit* as a "cookbook" for team building, selectively using activities that respond to their team's current need to boost morale, resolve conflict, etc. Using one or two activities by themselves is what we call a tactical application. Other readers will use *Building Team Spirit* as a resource for a comprehensive team development program over a six- to twelve-month period, systematically assessing and fostering team spirit through the learning activities in this volume. We call this use a strategic application. The Appendix materials are specifically designed to support the strategic use of the book in conjunction with the activities presented in Chapters 3 through 8.

Tactical Applications

If as a facilitator you are choosing one or two activities from this volume to address a specific team need, you may decide not to introduce teams to the Team Spirit Spiral, the structure of harmonics, or the background on spirited, high-performing teams treated in Chapters 1 and 2. You may also choose not to use the context-setting learning activities in Appendix D that help teams learn the six phases of the Team Spirit Spiral.

While it is useful for the facilitator to be grounded in the model, way of thinking, and language of team spirit presented in Chapters 1 and 2, you may not have the time or may elect not to introduce these distinctions to the team. Facilitators can choose activities pertinent to the needs of a team from the six phases of the Team Spirit Spiral:

1. Initiating (Chapter 3)
2. Visioning (Chapter 4)
3. Claiming (Chapter 5)
4. Celebrating (Chapter 6)
5. Letting Go (Chapter 7)
6. Service (Chapter 8)

For example, if your objective is:

To build morale

Choose Initiating and Celebrating learning activities from Chapters 3 and 6; these chapters are focused on creating relationship and acknowledging the good work performed by the team.

To resolve conflict

Choose Letting Go learning activities from Chapter 7 that foster straight, clear, forthright communication and respond to breakdowns between team members.

To encourage new thinking or planning for the future

Choose Visioning learning activities from Chapter 4 that help teams to create future team scenarios, as well as selected Service activities from Chapter 8 that deepen awareness of the importance of serving customers and the team.

To provide constructive feedback

Choose Letting Go learning activities from Chapter 7 that explicitly treat constructive feedback.

To clarify team roles and goals

Choose Claiming learning activities from Chapter 5 that provide structures for creating ownership and alignment of team goals and roles.

To encourage festivity and fun

Choose Celebrating learning activities from Chapter 6 for encouraging team animation and celebration.

Be sure to review the Learning Goals at the beginning of the activity and the What to Expect reflections at the end of the activity to clarify the purpose and scope of each activity. Should you decide that an assessment is needed to determine your selection, consult Appendices A and B and the last activity in Appendix E for assessment alternatives.

Strategic Applications

The first steps to effective work with a *mature team* are assessing the team's needs, identifying the phase or phases of the Spiral that are key to the team's spirit and performance, and recognizing the team's unique pattern of harmonics. Strategic applications of team spirit may usefully incorporate three critical resources provided for assisting facilitators in gathering data about the team:

1. Guidelines for Using the Team Spirit Assessment and Facilitating the Feedback and Action Planning Session in Appendix A is an in-depth, one-day feedback process, drawing on the Team Spirit Assessment, and an action planning phase that identifies next steps for the team to take to enhance team spirit.

2. Guidelines for Conducting Effective Team Interviews in Appendix B is a technique for getting data from a sample of team members through an interview process.

3. The Team Spirit Assessment activity in Appendix D is a two-hour experience that allows a team to reflect on its work together and to come to consensus about actions it can take to respond to its needs.

(See the last activity in Appendix E for further information about these assessment alternatives.)

While activities in Appendix D create the awareness of team spirit values and phases necessary to gain maximum benefit from the learning activities in Chapters 3 through 8, they also provide the facilitator with valuable feedback about the team. The context-setting activities help facilitators gain a better understanding of the personalities of team members and the dynamics and spirit present within the team.

Using data gathered about the team, the facilitator can choose a sequence of learning activities that will best serve the team. Chapters 3 through 8 provide learning activities specific to each of the phases of the Team Spirit Spiral.

For *start-up teams,* we recommend that the initial work with the team draw on context-setting activities from Appendix D. This foundation work is typically followed by the facilitation of activities selected from Chapters 3, 4, and 5 (that treat Initiating, Visioning, and Claiming). Start-up teams are not ready for the more interpersonal dimensions of Celebrating and Letting Go; they are more preoccupied with developing relationships, defining their purpose, and working out goals and roles. Therefore it is recommended that the Letting Go, Celebrating, and Service learning activities be done six to nine months later for these teams.

Mature teams have their own distinct dynamics that have arisen over time, and will accordingly require tailored applications of learning activities. The design and layout of team spirit activities should be adjusted to the needs of the team based upon assessment data gathered about the team. Even with mature teams it is useful to begin by doing context-setting activities from Appendix D.

It is recommended that facilitators and the teams they support commit a minimum of one year to the process of becoming a spirited team, working together periodically throughout the year. The notion that team development can be accomplished in an afternoon workshop is misguided. Team development requires ongoing commitment and attention to the spirit of the team. Team spirit can be used powerfully as a comprehensive team development program that nurtures growth and sustains the team throughout its process of becoming a high-performing team. After the first year, a readministration of the Team Spirit Assessment should be planned. The data from this reassessment will suggest additional work in selected phases of the Team Spirit Spiral.

SCENARIOS FOR USING TEAM SPIRIT ACTIVITIES

There are many combinations and permutations of activities, and ultimately the selection of activities will depend on a team's needs. The following scenarios suggest possible combinations of team spirit activities to address various team needs. Each scenario assumes a session length of four hours. Two activities are prescribed for each four-hour session, but the actual time for each activity varies widely. The number or letter following each activity indicates the chapter or appendix in which the activity is described in full.

A Newly-Formed Team That Can Commit to One Afternoon a Month for a One-Year Program of Development Using Team Spirit

As suggested previously, start-up teams naturally appreciate the support they gain from the first three phases of the Spiral during their initial months together. As they grow in their work together they require attention to the latter phases of the Spiral, Celebrating, Letting Go, and Service (six to nine months into the life of the team). Consequently, consider the following format of activities, beginning first with context-setting activities drawn from Appendix D and progressing through the phases of the Spiral in Chapters 3 through 8:

Session 1: Spirit Sayings [D] and Characteristics of Spirited Teams [D], creating awareness about spirited, high-performing teams, first from the perspective of current thinkers in this arena and secondly from the experiences of team members themselves.

Session 2: Personal Mandala [3] and Discovering the Harmonics That Underlie Spirit [D], providing an Initiating activity that fosters connection among team members and a further, deepening awareness of the Spiral and related harmonics.

Session 3: Personal Spiral [3] and Creating a Personal Vision:Dialogue with a Wisdom Figure [4], beginning with an Initiating activity that supports team members in exploring their relationship to the Spiral, then moving to Visioning, at the level of individual vision.

Session 4: Flight of Fancy [4] and Achieving a Spirit Leap in Enhancing Customer Service [4], providing the team with two frameworks for creating and clarifying their future.

Session 5: Reflection and discussion about the implications of the previous Visioning session and Team Mandala [4], allowing the team to visually express prized team values and visions.

Session 6: Personal Pathways [3] and Spirited Role Clarification [5], permitting the team to tell more of its story through additional Initiating work, and transitioning to Claiming in the role-clarification activity.

Session 7: Core Competencies of Team Members [5] and Spirited Team Accountability [5], serving to further the team's work in Claiming, first by considering competencies that members bring to the team and then by focusing on role alignment.

Session 8: Fostering Celebration: An Interview and Discussion Process [6] and Symbolizing Service [8], allowing the team to celebrate its greatness and to explore the essence of Service. (Note: The first activity requires that the facilitator conduct individual interviews prior to the group session.)

Session 9: Keys to the Kingdom [8] and Revealing the Spirit of Service— Individual [8], affording the team the opportunity to investigate archetypes of Service, probing individual motivations to serve.

Session 10: Letting Go through Constructive Feedback [7] and Identifying and Responding to Team Dissonances [7], allowing the team to develop skill at giving constructive feedback and to openly disclose dissonances that exist in the team.

Session 11: Insights from Athletic, Religious, Entertainment, and World Figures [7] and Celebration Teams [6], permitting the team to engage in a key Letting Go issue in a fun and nonthreatening way, culminating with a plan for Celebrating. (Note: Do only the celebration planning part of the Celebration Teams activity, reserving the last session for the actual celebrations.)

Session 12: Honoring Team Members [6] and Celebration Teams [6], serving to acknowledge and celebrate the value of both individual team members and the team as a whole.

At the conclusion of the twelfth session, it is useful to propose assessment work to assist the team in understanding its own unique patterns of consonances and dissonances and to plan succeeding activities that will support team spirit into year two. To this end, use the Team Spirit Assessment [Appendix D] and, if possible, engage the team in an in-depth feedback and action planning session [Appendix A].

A New Team Requiring Particular Emphasis on Relationship Building

Because of the newness of the team and because of the team's intention to foster relationship, this approach draws heavily on activities that create a context for team spirit and foster Initiating, with additional attention to Service and Visioning.

Session 1: Characteristics of Spirited Teams [2] and Walk in Nature: Discovering the Phases of the Spiral [2], providing perspectives on spirit from authorities in the field and familiarizing the team with the phases of the Team Spirit Spiral.

Session 2: Personal Mandala [3] and Team Wish List [3], facilitating greater connection and orientation for team members.

Session 3: Mountaintop Stories [3] and Revealing the Spirit of Service—Individual [8], fostering understanding among team members and an appreciation for their underlying willingness to serve.

Session 4: Flight of Fancy [4] and Revealing the Spirit of Service—Team [8], allowing the team to explore its future and to identify and name the underlying spirit of service operating in the team.

A Mature Team That Can Commit to One Afternoon a Month for a Year-Long Program of Development Using Team Spirit

Fostering team spirit in mature teams always calls for gathering data about team dynamics in relationship to the Team Spirit Spiral. This should be accomplished by following the interview format suggested in Appendix B. Based upon this preliminary data, recommendations can be made for the first several sessions. After the initial sessions have been completed, it is recommended that the Team Spirit Assessment be used to gather additional data, so you can further tailor the activities to the team's needs. For purposes of this scenario, assume the data gathered from the interview suggested some diminishment of vision and values and an absence of relationship among highly diverse members, preventing the team from effectively bonding together.

Session 1: Spirit Sayings [D] and Characteristics of Spirited Teams [D], creating awareness about spirited, high-performing teams, first from the perspective of current organizational thinkers and secondly from the experiences of team members themselves.

Session 2: Personal Mandala [3] and The Seasons of a Team's Life: Establishing Team Climate [D], providing an Initiating activity that fosters connection among team members and a further awareness of the phases of the Spiral.

Session 3: A Values Activity: Rites of Passage [4] and Achieving a Spirit Leap in Enhancing Customer Service [4], fostering values formation and new potential for serving customers.

Session 4: Spirit Walk [3] and Team Mandala [4], promoting understanding about team member diversity and assisting the team in visually representing prized vision and values.

Session 5: Symbol of Service [8] and Team Spirit Assessment [D], creating awareness of individual interpretations of Service and providing data about the team's relationship to the Team Spirit Spiral. (For the following sessions in this scenario, assume that this data revealed the need for additional Claiming work necessitated by a realignment of team vision as a result of earlier activities, along with issues regarding withheld communication related to the completion of a difficult project—that is, Letting Go issues.)

Session 6: A Letting Go Ritual [7] and Spirited Team Accountability [5], allowing team members to accept the ending of a recent project and to clarify critical team accountability.

Session 7: Identifying and Responding to Team Dissonances [7] and Spirited Role Clarification [5], fostering the team's capacity to acknowledge and respond to its dissonance and to focus team roles.

Session 8: Letting Go through Constructive Feedback [7] and Service Circle [8], supporting the team in developing constructive feedback skills and exploring the meaning of Service.

Session 9: Claiming Organization Support [5] and Identifying Team Member Skill Sets and Mind-Sets [5], helping the team to gain needed organization support and to claim critical skills necessary to perform its work.

Session 10: Getting Out of the Box Exercise [7] and Dialogue with an Imaginary Guru [7], fostering new understanding about team dissonances and possibilities for responding to a difficult relationship with a colleague.

Session 11: Meeting Your Inner Servant [8] and Celebration Teams [6], permitting the team to explore its personal sense of Service through a visualization, culminating with a plan for Celebrating. (Note: Do only the celebration planning part of the Celebration Teams activity, reserving the last session for the actual celebrations.)

Session 12: Honoring Team Members [6] and Celebration Teams [6], serving to acknowledge and celebrate the value of both individual team members and the team as a whole.

A New Cross-Functional Team That Must Complete Its Task in Six Months and Can Only Devote Two Afternoon Sessions to Team Spirit (in a Firm Employing a Comprehensive, Strategic Application of Team Spirit)

In this scenario a strategic application of team spirit is assumed. Accordingly, all teams in the organization participate in a company-wide introduction to team spirit that consists of two afternoon sessions. The four activities used in these two half-day sessions for all employees were as follows:

Characteristics of Spirited Teams [D]

Discovering the Harmonics That Underlie Spirit [D]

The Seasons of a Team's Life: Establishing Team Climate [D]

Revealing the Spirit of Service—Individual [8]

Based upon this common foundation and depending on whether the team is a start-up or mature team, activities are tailored to the needs of each team. For this scenario assume the situation involves a start-up task force.

Session 1: Personal Mandala [3] and Team Wish List [3], fostering relationship and clarifying expectations among team members.

Session 2: Team Mandala [4] and Core Competencies of Team Members [5], creating a visual representation of the team's vision and working toward a common understanding of team roles.

A New Cross-Functional Team That Must Complete Its Task in Six Months and Can Devote Two Afternoon Sessions to Team Spirit (in a Firm That Has Endorsed the Use of Team Spirit in Tactical Applications)

In this scenario the task force did not have the luxury of an orientation to team spirit. Therefore, the two afternoon experiences must accomplish a great deal in very little time. Assume in this scenario that the situation involves a start-up team.

Session 1: Characteristics of Spirited Teams [D], a brief lecturette on the Team Spirit Spiral, and Personal Mandala [3], clarifying the phases of the Team Spirit Spiral and building team relationship.

Session 2: Team Mandala [4] and Spirited Team Accountability [5], creating a visual representation of the team's vision and working toward a common understanding of team roles.

TIPS ON FACILITATING ALL TYPES OF TEAMS

It is useful to follow certain protocols delivering team spirit activities, irrespective of team type and team needs. Whether the team is new or mature, initial conversations with the team leader, team liaison, or several team members regarding team needs and goals will be invaluable for establishing relationship, answering questions, and creating the context for the use of the team spirit activities.

When using team spirit activities over time, vary the method for creating subteams for activities that require small groups. Arbitrarily assign persons seated together to subteams for some of the activities, and ask participants to randomly count off for other activities.

Team spirit is designed to take place in the lives of the team, during the intervals between team spirit sessions. Therefore, routinely ask the team to discuss how team spirit is making a difference in their work; ask for concrete examples. Allow for Letting Go issues to be fully expressed, as well as gains in team effectiveness; record both consonant and dissonant responses on a flip chart. Encourage the team to post the Team Spirit Spiral in a prominent place in their workspace and to actively use the Spiral phases and the structure of harmonics as a way to make sense of their work relationships and progress in becoming a great team.

RESPONDING TO QUESTIONS ABOUT THE "SPIRIT" IN TEAM SPIRIT

Typically team participants are receptive to team spirit activities. Many participants will initially understand team spirit to be the kind of "rah-rah" associated with cheerleading or athletic events. Over time they come to understand and appreciate the deeper implication of team spirit as it is associated with high-performing teams. Rarely do team members confuse spirit for religion.

Facilitators should be prepared to respond to questions about team spirit. The following perspectives may be useful to draw upon when responding to questions about the "spirit" in team spirit:

- Team spirit is about developing high-performing teams and organizations.
- The research on high-performing teams suggests that team members routinely refer to a spirit that is present and operates within their midst, moving them to produce extraordinary results.
- This book provides a model—the Team Spirit Spiral—that concretely identifies the phases and qualities of spirit that lead to high performance.
- Team spirit is a quality of energy and exuberance that operates in great teams, that catapults these teams to high levels of performance.
- Extensive use of team spirit in large, small, for-profit, and non-profit organizations has demonstrated the effectiveness of team spirit in fostering high-performing teams.

TEAM SPIRIT IS FOCUSED ON BEING, NOT DOING

The learning activities in this volume are designed to enable individuals, teams, and organizations to discern, experience, and influence spirit that is at the heart of high performance. As participants engage in the learning activities, they gain insights that foster new levels of understanding and lead to changes in behavior in their personal lives and in their team and organizational environments. They learn new ways of relating and interconnecting. They learn to "be" team spirit. They become sensitized to the old saying, "It's not what you do, but how you do it that is important." How you do it is determined by who you are "being" when you do it.

Building Team Spirit grew out of a program for team and organization development offered by the Expanded Learning Institute. For more information on the Team Spirit Program and the four-day Certification Program, see page 391.

Part I

PERSPECTIVES ON BUILDING TEAM SPIRIT

1

Spirit in High-Performing Teams and the Team Spirit Spiral

Whatever else high performance and excellence may be based on,
they would seem to have something to do with the quality of spirit
...human Spirit, our Spirit, the Spirit of our organizations.
Harrison Owen

DISPIRITED TEAMS: THE CONTEXT

Many modern organizations have lost their spirit, even their interest in spirit. They operate with vision and value structures that only faintly stir the hearts and souls of their employees. When heart and soul are missing, workers may withdraw or compensate through compulsive, frenetic, obsessive, or addictive behaviors. These organizations merely keep up with current demands, providing meager service. They are often wounded and in pain, unable to foster authentic communication or to heal themselves. They are without spirit and without joy.

At the same time, organizations have perfected their technological prowess, their analytical capacities for making decisions and improving processes, and their form and structure. Great efficiencies have been realized, but at the same time organizations are numbed-out and glazed over. They have lost touch with their spirit.

The technological age has fostered an information explosion, with the amount of available information increasing at a staggering rate. We venerate and worship technology. But a certain emptiness pervades our organizations. The deeper meaning of our work has become remote and inaccessible. Our concept of who we are and what we can become has been lost with our spirit.

Ironically, it is the new science that teaches us about the vast unseen that operates below the level of form and structure (Wheatley, 1992). We know that atoms are manifestations of energy. Only recently has our thinking about teams and organizations acknowledged the energy, the spirit, that underlies high-performing teams and organizations.

A NEW WAY OF FOSTERING TEAMS IS CALLED FORTH

Efforts to unite spirit and teams and organizations arise out of research on high-performing systems that identifies spirit as a key underlying consideration in great teams and organizations (Vaill, 1989). High-performing organizations are calling forth an approach to work that stirs and touches the souls of those who make up the organization, generating unbounded enthusiasm for extraordinary service. The call is for individuals to go beyond themselves, so that the team's results are more than the sum of the individuals' potential. What is called for is relating and working together in a spirited way, so that teams inspire bolder and more imaginative responses to the challenges confronting organizations.

Exponential gains in organization effectiveness are possible when teams are infused with spirit. Despite the potency of this synergy of team and spirit, the notion is still incompletely understood by modern enterprises. Realizing the possibility of spirited, high-performing teams requires a shift in awareness, a shift in values, and a shift in the way teams work. This book provides, in Chapters 3 through 8, the tools, resources, learning activities, and interventions to nurture team spirit.

THE INTERPLAY OF ORGANIZATION, SCIENCE, AND SPIRIT

There is a growing appreciation of the concept that the seemingly opposite considerations of organization, science, and spirit are interdependent and mutually inclusive. The approach to team development described in these pages integrates thinking about spirit with current thought about team and organization development, as well as thinking about science. The synthesis that serves as the basis for the model of team development identified in these pages includes:

Organization: Contemporary thinking from the field of organizational development about how teams move through developmental phases and can be cultivated to work more effectively.

Science: Disciplined scientific investigation of life, from the smallest organism to the universe itself, that has revealed similar and identifiable evolutionary patterns.

Spirit: The urge to find meaning and purpose and the interconnections between human beings that are important to people around the world and across time.

These three areas may seem divergent, yet they share a common core. Each creates wholeness out of separateness; each offers a unique contribution to the process of bonding that must occur before a team can function at a high performance level.

The Team as a Series of Organizational Stages

Often, we think of a team as a thing created at a moment in time. Since the earliest moments of humankind, men and women gathered together in community to hunt, to harvest, and to prepare meals; these human endeavors served naturally to create teams. Consider also the possibility that teams not only are created, but also evolve.

In 1988, team development consultants Allan Drexler and David Sibbett expanded upon the groundbreaking research done by Jack Gibb in the early 1950s. They conceptualized a team development model called the "team performance system." Drexler and Sibbett suggested that all teams pass through stages of development. Each stage presents the team with particular concerns. For each stage, Drexler and Sibbett describe the behaviors that signal whether the concerns peculiar to that stage have been resolved. If such concerns are not resolved, the team is "stuck" at that stage, requiring resolution before it can move on to later stages.

Drexler and Sibbett facilitated team development based upon this model. Teams and organizations benefited from having a shared model and vocabulary from which they could understand the phases and stages of their development as a team. From Sibbett and Drexler, *Building Team Spirit* draws the idea that a team is something that evolves over time, with necessary phases that lead to team effectiveness. *Building Team Spirit* also acknowledges the importance of a shared model and vocabulary that teams can draw upon to understand and enhance their work together.

The Team as a Life-Giving Force Understood by Science

Living things are commonly at odds with themselves. As a simple example, we'd like to be on time for work but we'd like to sleep in. In 1992, Margaret Wheatley, drawing upon the work of general systems theorist Eric Jantsch, wrote about this disequilibrium (referred to as "dissonance" in the next chapter) that she affirmed as inherently life-giving and nurturing. The acceptance and resolution of dissonance, Wheatley argues, is the process that permits systems to regenerate and move to higher levels of awareness and effectiveness. Eric Jantsch calls this process "self-organization."

Every team is similar to a living organism. At every moment in time it has its own blend of forces, some consonant and some dissonant. Teams do not evolve by suppressing their dissonance; rather, they move to higher levels of effectiveness by understanding and embracing it.

From Margaret Wheatley, *Building Team Spirit* takes the idea that the disequilibrium within a team or organization provides an energy source capable of moving the organization to a higher level of awareness and effectiveness. It is this disequilibrium that we must learn to embrace. The value structure that undergirds team spirit, to be presented in Chapter 2, identifies dissonant, as well as consonant, factors that operate within the dynamics of a team.

The Team as an Expression of Human Spirit

Matthew Fox, a key investigator of spirit in work, integrates ideas from ancient traditions with more recent thinking about spirit (1994). Fox points to native and traditional peoples' capacity to recognize and celebrate "awe and wonder" as a group experience. Further, he emphasizes the cleansing force that comes from recognizing the darker, more difficult manifestations of the group experience.

We can be brought to vivid awareness of these two values through a process Fox calls "creation storytelling." Such storytelling grounds us in a history of how we arrived at our present, awakens within us awe and wonder at the fact of our being here, and permits the "letting go" that is the expression of the dissonant elements of the group experience. We will return to the importance of storytelling in Chapter 2. In addition, many of the learning activities that appear throughout this volume serve as vehicles for teams to tell their stories.

Fox says the path that the spirit takes "...is a path away from the superficial into the depths; away from the outer person into the inner person; away from the privatized and individualistic into the deeply communitarian." Through Matthew Fox, *Building Team Spirit* lays claim to the importance of transcendence, the team's capacity to share "awe and wonder" and the capacity for cleansing that lies within the group. *Building Team Spirit* explicitly identifies the importance of celebrating and forthright communication to team effectiveness.

AT THE HEART OF HIGH-PERFORMING TEAMS: SPIRIT

Just as scientists have revealed atomic particles as the unseen but essential building blocks of the physical universe, the unseen but essential qualities (or phases) of team spirit can be identified and named. The defining characteristic of the high-performing team—the trait that makes a team more than the sum of its members—is this unseen but critical "spirit."

The elusive quality of spirit can be experienced through the learning activities used in *Building Team Spirit*. For example, with a little prompting team members will recall nearly-forgotten experiences of extraordinary teams, teams full of spirit, in which they have participated. They take great delight in doing this, creating greater consciousness about the possibility of team spirit. (See Appendix D, Characteristics of Spirited Teams, for an activity to facilitate this awareness of spirited, high-performing teams.)

The activities help team members understand that spirit is not separate from worldly affairs, nor is spirit some ephemeral or ambiguous state. It is at the core of our humanity, should we choose to notice and cultivate it. We can become more conscious of spirit in work.

Spirit is the committed exploration of personal meaning and purpose in life and work. It inspires us. It draws us beyond ourselves. When we go beyond ourselves, spirit and teams come together. Out of selflessness we give ourselves freely to important work, to the service of others, or to colleagues with whom we join in work. High-performing teams exhibit selflessness and a sense of spirit.

In moving beyond narrow self interest, beyond the individualism that permeates our culture, the possibility of extraordinary teams emerges. Spirit is at the core of this possibility, and team spirit is the desired end state.

While at some level spirit defies cognitive understanding, we can name the qualities of spirit operating in teams. Identifying these qualities can provide a common vocabulary for teams to talk about their work together. Consider the following six qualities that we characterize as "phases" of a spiral in Figure 1-1.

All teams, whether consciously or unconsciously, move through and operate in all phases, linked by the critical sixth integrating component: Service. Each phase has its own unique contribution to make in realizing spirit in a team. These phases spiral together simultaneously and interdependently. Our experience shows that ordinary work groups can become spirited, high-performing teams by consciously attending to each of these

The core integrating phase of Service

Quality of spirit: The team experiences contribution and service to customers and to the team.

Letting Go phase

Quality of spirit: A sense of freedom and completion arises from being forthright and sharing with full integrity.

Celebrating phase

Quality of spirit: There is a presence of awe, wonder, and an appreciation for the contribution of the team and team members.

Claiming phase

Quality of spirit: The team experiences solidarity, single-minded purpose, and assurance about what needs to be accomplished.

Visioning phase

Quality of spirit: An extraordinary sense of possibility for what can be created is alive and present for the team.

Initiating phase

Quality of spirit: A profound sense of relationship exists, wherein team members feel belonging and trust in their work together.

Note: The qualities of spirit represented in the Spiral interact in complex ways, as they blend and fuse throughout the life of the team. For example, the Letting Go quality of spirit is ideally occurring in every phase of the team's work together.

Figure 1-1. The Team Spirit Spiral

phases. The learning activities provided in this volume support teams in recognizing the phases of the Spiral and thus engaging in the conscious development of spirited, high-performing teams. Building team spirit is a dynamic, evolving, organic process.

Chapter 2 explores the phases of the Team Spirit Spiral in more detail.

The Harmonics of Team Spirit

*Organizations lack...faith, faith that they can accomplish
their purposes in various ways
and that they do best when they focus on direction and vision,
letting transient forms emerge and disappear.
We seem fixated on structures; and we build them strong and complex
because we must, we believe, hold back the dark forces that are out to destroy us...
The things we fear most in organizations—fluctuations, disturbances,
imbalances—need not be signs of an impending disorder that will destroy us.
Instead, fluctuations are the primary source of creativity.*
Margaret Wheatley

This chapter explores storytelling as a means of sharing the values and spirit of the team. It also describes the harmonics, consonant and dissonant pairs, operating within each phase of the Spiral.

CREATING SPIRIT IN TEAMS THROUGH STORYTELLING

Storytelling is a powerful tool. Many of the learning activities in this volume are designed so that team members can tell their stories. In telling their stories, team members and the team reveal their spirit. We coach those we work with not only to tell their stories but to listen attentively to the stories that the team tells, to the deep currents within the stories.

Great teams do not forget the stories that reveal their soul, their traditions, their spirit and mystery of everyday experiences. In the following pages I relate stories of spirited, high-performing teams I have led or worked with and of persons who give us clues about each phase identified in the Team Spirit Spiral.

Service

Service is at the heart of the spiral. The team exists to serve its customers.

Nineteen years ago I led a spirited team working in an urban college to create alternative programs for adults. The team's passion was to create new modes of teaching and learning that would attract new learners to the campus. In challenging the status quo, the team often found itself in conflict with faculty members who were reluctant to part with traditional ideas about teaching and learning. That team's passion to serve adults changed the college's notion of service, as the team provided adult learners with more flexible teaching and learning approaches centered around the learners' lives and career pursuits.

Initiating

Theologian David Steindl-Rast suggests that spirit is ultimately about belonging and connectedness. The Initiating phase of the spiral captures the importance of relationships.

I asked members of a mature team to "tell their story" by creating personal mandalas (see Chapter 3, Personal Mandala). Mandala is the Sanskrit word for circle. A mandala, particularly common in Asia, visually symbolizes the heartfelt values of a family or group.

These technically skilled people groaned aloud when I asked them to create their mandala without using words. I asked for images and visual representations symbolizing the following statements that were written in the four quadrants of a circle:

A gift I bring to the team.
A source of personal pride.
My frustration with the team.
My team spirit goal.

They worked slowly and intently using red, blue, green, pink, and yellow markers to create their images. Energy peaked when team members began to present their mandalas. One commented, "I've worked with this team for over ten years but never really knew what my colleagues were proud of in their lives."

Initiating, the initial rite of passage for a team, supports the development of belonging and trust. Stories of initiating say: "This is who *I* am. This is who *we* are." These stories ease and transform feelings of tentativeness, imbalance, awkwardness, and disconnectedness that a new team may experience.

Visioning

Music, especially jazz, brings me congruence, awareness, and an experience of life that other forms of expression—poetry, cooking, painting, gardening, etc.—do not. Among jazz artists, Miles Davis is one of my favorites. Davis' playing, especially in the 60s, was characterized by a certain sparseness. He used notes and phrases sparingly, in contrast to the rapid-fire barrages of notes played by his contemporaries. Critics in the jazz world observed that Davis' uniqueness appeared in the spaces between his notes.

Most teams focus on the notes themselves—on form, organization charts, computer systems, project plans, and role descriptions. With this focus they miss the essence that generates extraordinary results. Davis admonished his band, *"Don't play what's there. Play what's not there. Don't play what you know. Play what you don't know."* Like jazz groups, teams grow by exploring the unknown and unleashing their possibilities. As Davis believed, we limit our contribution by playing what we know; we expand our contribution by playing music we have never heard.

Stories of Visioning clarify purpose, core values, and beliefs and point to a future of better service. The spirit of Visioning lies in remembering, being present to, and establishing what the team is capable of contributing to others.

Claiming

Claiming gives power to the vision. Through Claiming, a team takes ownership of its goals as members and as a group. Claiming establishes the team's path on the journey to extraordinary Service.

Claiming pulls together the needed resources to fulfill the Vision. Spirit is expressed through the commitment, resolve, and solidarity accomplished in the Claiming phase.

A product development organization that I worked with was reorganized into self-directed teams. The level of autonomy created anxiety. A key member of the team, Peter, asked, "How will we be able to formulate goals without a leader to point the way?"

Rosemary shared, "I feel uneasy. At times, I want to express my support for a particular idea, but I don't want my colleagues to think I'm pushy." Jose declared, "I have been doing data gathering for ten years without a hitch. Now I am expected to understand everything about product development."

The organization supported this team during the transition period. Initiating and Visioning learning activities helped team members to appreciate their uniqueness and opened possibilities. After an initial period of uncertainty and disarray team members started to "claim" how they wanted to contribute to the team.

Peter observed, "If we can incorporate Rosemary's comments on the difficulties she faces with her role, I think we can improve our whole process." Jonathan acknowledged, "While I feel unsure about performing more varied roles, I enjoy the greater breadth of responsibility with the new team orientation." Rosemary said, "I am working harder than I ever have, but I enjoy the greater range of our new roles."

From these new work patterns, greater team interdependency emerged. Results followed: first, an increase in product innovations; later, an increase in customer satisfaction. The group had successfully begun the job of transforming their work together as a team.

Through stories of claiming, individuals take ownership of their team roles. Claiming stories create affinity between the individual and the group.

Celebrating

In the mid 1980's I watched a video teleconference on coaching as a management skill. Participants included a half-dozen professional athletes, paired with the coaches with whom they had worked. UCLA's Johnny Wooden was matched with Kareem Abdul Jabbar and Bill Russell of the Boston Celtics was paired with his coach, Red Auerbach, among other pairs of coaches and players.

I was taken by the infectious level of recognition that was communicated between players and players, coaches and coaches, and coaches and players. Johnny Wooden acknowledged Red Auerbach for a play Auerbach initiated in the 1950's that changed the way he thought about basketball; Kareem acknowledged Bill Russell for his great moves as a center. Auerbach recognized Bill's commitment to the game, etc., etc.

One could argue that with great players and great coaches it is easy to find much to acknowledge. But which came first? The acknowledgment, or the greatness? Or are they mutually reinforcing?

Stories of celebrating create an experience of aliveness and vibrancy in teams. Celebration stories make apparent the spirit operating in a team, through energy, awe, and wonder about the team and what the team is accomplishing.

Letting Go

Recently I watched two teams debrief after a long, arduous project. They seemed lifeless and uninterested as they talked about what worked. There was a tone of dispiritedness, of resignation.

Then one team member spoke of the resentment prompted by long hours and unclear expectations. Another expressed irritation that at key points the team failed to lay claim to its work. A third member said the team's mutual support had broken down at times, once, in a way that was very embarrassing to her. Others joined in. It was like hearing fragmented and unspoken sentences complete themselves. As the unspoken was spoken, the room became more alive.

Letting Go is accepting and acting upon the permission to tell the truth. Stories of Letting Go affirm that feedback is not only acceptable, it is safe and welcomed. Letting Go stories drop the facade and provide a safe space for what needs to be said, no matter how difficult.

The stories that teams tell arouse curiosity, evoke emotions, and clarify aspirations. The stories teams tell trace rites of passage, trials, initiation, wonder, and the underlying meaning of the team's work together. The stories of the team and organization create order and wholeness out of randomness and enhance movement through the phases of the Spiral generating trust and respect among team members.

VALUES UNDERLYING TEAM SPIRIT: CONSONANCES AND DISSONANCES

Using music as a metaphor for building team spirit provides a way to understand group values and dynamics. Each phase of the Team Spirit Spiral has its own unique harmonics combining both consonant factors and dissonant factors. Just as in great music, teams are animated and enlivened by drawing on *both* consonances and dissonances.

Most teams welcome the consonant—for example, the sense of security that comes from working with long-term associates, agreement about a key role to be performed, or the alignment of team energies in accomplishing shared vision and goals.

Most teams avoid the dissonant—dissonant voices say: "We're not doing this right." "That doesn't work for me." "I'm not happy with this." "I am disappointed that we did not produce the result we anticipated."

In music, dissonance leads to resolution. In teams, embracing the dissonance can move the team to a position of strength, ultimately leading to a more spirited team and to heightened service.

The dynamic of team growth can be seen as a continual ebb and flow, as the team embraces and builds upon consonances while acknowledging and working through dissonances at each phase of the Spiral.

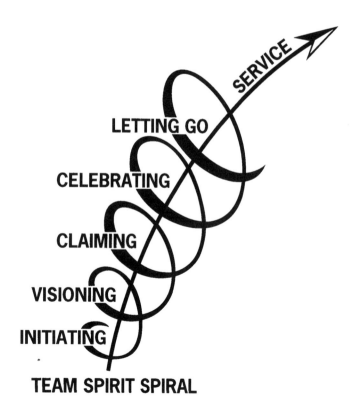

CONSONANCES

(a combination of musical tones that have resolved—that is, they are in agreement)

Service
-*contribution*: generously and freely giving to another
-*aligned execution*: fulfilling, in a unified way, customer and team needs
-*mutual support*: providing reciprocal assistance

Initiating
-*orientation*: becoming familiarized and aware
-*belonging*: feeling allied with and a part of the team
-*trust*: feeling reliant and secure about team members

Visioning
-*shared vision/values*: agreeing on what is possible and its underlying worth and merit
-*compassion*: experiencing empathy and concern for another
-*presence*: deeply experiencing the purpose of the team

Claiming
-*goal/role alignment*: agreeing on the outcome and the means for achieving it
-*organization support*: securing the necessary resources from the organization
-*competence*: developing skills and awareness needed to perform team roles

Celebrating
-*appreciation*: feeling recognized and acknowledged
-*energy*: experiencing vitality and aliveness
-*wonder*: experiencing an unbounded sense of possibility

Letting Go
-*disclosure*: revealing previously suppressed attitudes and opinions
-*constructive feedback*: providing forthright responses that encourage growth
—*completion*: feeling a sense of freedom when everything has been said

DISSONANCES

(a combination of unresolved musical tones)

Service
-*depletion*: feeling used up, unable to freely give to another
-*uncoordinated action*: incompletely fulfilling customer and team needs
-*unsupportiveness*: acting without concern for others

Initiating
-*disorientation*: experiencing disequilibrium and fear
-*alienation*: feeling like a misfit, not a part of the team
-*mistrust*: feeling insecure and cautious about team members

Visioning
-*ambiguous vision/values*: experiencing uncertainty about what is possible—let alone its underlying worth and merit
-*callousness*: being insensitive and harsh
-*aridness*: feeling barren and empty, without a sense of purpose

Claiming
-*nonalignment*: disagreeing about the outcome and means for achieving it
-*nonsupport*: being unable to secure the necessary resources from the organization
-*deficiency*: not having the skills and awareness needed to perform team roles

Celebrating
-*nonappreciation*: not feeling recognized and acknowledged
-*burnout*: feeling used up and ineffective in the team
-*disenchantment*: feeling repelled and put out

Letting Go
-*withheld communication*: concealing attitudes and opinions from others
-*criticism*: offering unsupportive critical feedback
-*incompletion*: feeling regretful about withholding communications

EXPLORING THE PHASES OF THE TEAM SPIRIT SPIRAL

Team Spirit weaves the common threads running through organizational, scientific, and spiritual thought into a dynamic model for creating "high-performance" teams. At the core of the Team Spirit Spiral is Service, acknowledging that the team exists to serve its customers. The Team Spirit model is built on the premise that a high-performance team has at its heart a spirit that is felt, shared, and honored by all team members. This spirit manifests itself in the sense of pride experienced by the team as it discovers its power to provide extraordinary service.

In order to achieve high performance, the team needs to function as a harmonious unit. Such harmony is a result of recognizing, celebrating, and drawing energy from the concordant aspects of the team, such as the excitement of sharing a vision or the feeling of comfort and security derived from working with long-time friends or coworkers. Harmony is refined by recognizing, confronting, and transforming discordant aspects of the team, such as feelings of powerlessness in the face of a seemingly impossible dilemma or a breakdown in group trust or communication.

The interplay of harmonics (i.e., consonances and dissonances in the team) at each phase of Team Spirit Spiral is briefly explained in the following paragraphs. The existence of dissonance in a phase is an indication that the facilitator should place emphasis on assisting the team's work on that phase. For example, a team struggling with the Initiating or new formation phase will benefit greatly from the activities in Chapter 3.

Service

Service is at the core of the Team Spirit Spiral. Delighting customers and contributing to others is essential to high-performing teams. Extraordinary Service arises out of the successful work the team has done in the Initiating, Visioning, and Claiming phases of the Spiral. Service includes making products or services that enrich the worlds of other individuals, internal departments, or organizations. Consonant factors associated with Service include committed action that leads to significant contribution to customers, and joy, passion, and delight in ministering to those served by the team. Successful Service reflects a splendid realization of visions and an experience of mutual support and contribution by team members and customers.

Dissonant signs that indicate the need for team development include feelings of lack of support, depletion of energy among team members, or uncoordinated action in the delivery of Service.

Initiating

Individuals called together in teams often feel shaken during team formation. This dissonant quality is to be expected. It is healthy. It can sensitize team members to individual needs and the needs of the team as a whole. These needs include understanding the purpose of the team and the contribution each team member might make to the realization of that purpose.

When a team successfully engages in Initiating work, members of the team achieve the consonant qualities of belonging, positive orientation, and mutual trust. These feelings permeate the team, empowering it to define and accomplish its work effectively.

Signs of dissonance in the form of mistrust, fear, or disorientation among team members indicate a need for the team to work through some of the learning activities on Initiating.

Visioning

Visioning and Initiating are highly interdependent phases of the Spiral, and for some teams Visioning may precede the work of Initiating. The solid base of relationship that Initiating provides allows a powerful basis for Visioning, but the reverse is also true. Visioning engages the team in consideration of the essence of its work. The team distinguishes current reality from the ideal reality (i.e., vision) it holds for the future. Visioning results in consonance as the team clarifies its purpose, core values, and beliefs, and develops a most extraordinary future sense of how customers might be served. As a result of successful Visioning the team is excited about the possibilities of their work together.

When vision and values are unclear, dissonance occurs within teams. Such dissonant factors as callousness regarding those the team serves and ambiguous vision or values suggest the need to revisit the Visioning phase. The dissonant experience of emptiness or aridness within the team conveys that the team is not "present" to its possibility to serve generously.

Claiming

The development of team relationships and the team vision experienced in the first two phases of the Spiral lead to Claiming. Claiming involves the team's taking ownership of goals and roles for its work together, based upon shared vision and values.

Consonant factors associated with Claiming include: alignment of team members with the goals of the team, commitment to the growth and development of team members, ownership of team roles, and the team's capacity to secure needed organizational support.

When the team's work in Claiming is dissonant, typical signs include invalidation of the team or the work it undertakes, feelings of inadequacy, and lack of agreement regarding goals or roles.

Celebrating

Successful Service results in Celebrating. The spirit of the team is ignited and nurtured in Celebrating. This phase of the Spiral is life-giving and nurtures the further work of the team. It provides a sense of unity and spirit.

Consonant factors operating within the Celebrating phase include feelings of being appreciated and acknowledged within the team and a sense of unbounded energy, the capacity to "move mountains." Celebrating is characterized by a sense of wonder that pervades the team, generating a desire to "do it again."

When team members feel unappreciated, disenchanted, or burned out, it is important that teams recognize the resulting "dis-ease" and respond to the dissonance, creating the missing sense of appreciation and spirit within the team. Such transformations may arise through work in the final phase of the Spiral, Letting Go.

Letting Go

The consonant factors characteristic of a successful Letting Go phase are forthrightness, disclosure, and constructive feedback, freely given and received. These characteristics are not only acceptable in the team, but safely practiced and welcomed.

When the team experiences dissonance in the form of withheld communication or tension and disintegration in relationships, it is a signal to the team to find ways to begin Letting Go. Letting Go allows for new beginnings, for initiation, for a future not based in the past.

Breakdowns occur in the best teams. An array of dissonances can develop within the team. Team members experience disappointment when the intended service is *not* provided. Team members can become frustrated with the performance of other team members or others in the organization. Conflict can occur as a result of committed team members having honest differences of opinion about how best to serve the customer. In short, there is a dark side even in quite successful teams. Although our experience of it may be agitation, anxiety, sadness, or anger, this dark side offers creative opportunities.

If we value embracing and confronting the problems in a constructive way, rather than withholding feelings or repressing differences, Letting Go can be powerfully transforming. The key is to provide the space, time, safety, and opportunity for "truth telling" within the team.

Significant forces work against spirit in teams. Years of conditioning elevate and enshrine individualism. Organizations exalt form and structure, relegating the unseen, the spirit of the team, to unconsciousness. Organizations ignore or respond ineptly to the needs of the spirit. Intolerant of problems and ambiguity, organizations rely on aggressive individuals or on form and structure to find their healing and purpose. It isn't there.

We believe that embracing team spirit, in all of its various manifestations—both its light and its shadow—is critical to significant team and organization renewal.

The Team Spirit Spiral provides guidance for developing inspired, high-performing individuals, as well as teams and organizations. The phases of the Team Spirit Spiral identify the paths that individuals can take to enhance consonances and identify and work through personal dissonances (see Chapter 3, Personal Spiral). As teams work through the activities in this book, they will become more sensitive to the consonances and dissonances in their own lives as well as the team's life.

Part II

LEARNING ACTIVITIES FOR NURTURING TEAM SPIRIT

3

Initiating Strong Team Relationships

*We in the corporate setting tend to believe that we are
supposed to check our deepest personal selves—our inner lives,
our soul's development—at the door of the workplace, at least publicly.
This assumption prevents us from bringing some
of the most powerful and creative parts of ourselves to our jobs.
In corporations, fear, anxiety, a sense of isolation, apathy,
and despair are the results of spiritual poverty...*
Barbara Shipka

Modern enterprises can learn from traditional and native cultures that include belief in the collective spirit. When members of the tribe worked together effectively the spirit of the tribe was filled with wonder, awe, and clear purpose. When individuals in the tribe disassociated from or devalued the collective, the spirit waned. Modern enterprises are unaware of the spirit of the whole, preferring instead "rugged individualism"—which draws energy away from the collective and results in separateness and diminished results.

Rugged individualism in our modern society has led to a loss of trust and belonging. We yearn for the sense of community we once had in neighborhoods, families, and churches. As workplaces have commanded increasing prominence in the lives of men and women, they have generally failed to supply the missing balance between individual and community.

Modern enterprises assume that workers will demonstrate the trust and belonging that are necessary to good team relationships. They miss the point that the deep connection and relationship that their members long for requires the creation of an environment where relationships and the spirit of the team can flower.

The current emphasis on teams is a hopeful sign as it has begun to nudge us out of our self-focused, egocentric orientation. We have begun to understand that great teams honor both individual members (the parts) *and* the transcending collective (the whole). Great teams are characterized by a merging and fusing of individual energy into something greater, going beyond the bounds of individual ego and self.

Modern enterprises are unclear about how to foster the transcending collective and the requisite trust and belonging necessary to restore the spirit of the enterprise. They have few team rituals or traditions for initiating such relationship and connection. Acknowledgment of high performance and extraordinary service requires such rituals.

The Initiating phase of a team's work responds to the possibility of merging and fusing the energy of team members into a collective whole. The team's work together in the Initiating phase is about belonging and trust. Trust requires that we open ourselves to others. The opposite of trust is control and manipulation.

This phase of the Spiral is a rite of passage. It requires a willingness to respond to the call, a crossing over the threshold to create wholeness out of separateness. The learning activities in this chapter support the critical Initiating work of the team.

The activities in this chapter are designed to be used with teams that are forming for the first time, although it is just as important to use these activities with mature teams that may have neglected the Initiating phase of the Spiral. Even in the best of mature teams, trust and feelings of belonging may need to be reestablished, perhaps at a deeper level of intimacy.

It is also important that a team give attention to Initiating when a change or an addition of a new team member occurs. When such changes take place the team as a whole is returned to the Initiating phase of the Spiral, creating the circumstances for using the activities in this chapter. If you are facilitating a group formed for only a short duration, whether a week or a few months, use one or more Initiating activities to foster strong relationships, belonging, and trust.

Initiating is important regardless of the duration of the team's work together. This chapter provides learning activities for start-up teams, mature teams, teams in the midst of change, and teams organized for a short duration or a single task.

The Learning Activities

Personal Mandala involves each team member in creating a mandala, a visual rendering of cherished beliefs and values that tells each individual's story.

Personal Spiral helps individual team members to discern their own spirit and path through the Spiral.

Spirit Walk helps team members appreciate the diversity of their membership.

Personal Pathways allows members of the team to tell the stories of their lives and career pathways that led them to this team.

Mountaintop Stories builds connection and relationship among team participants based upon stories of importance to the lives of team members.

Play Your Own Kind of Music assists the team in defining its core values using the structure of harmonics presented in Chapter 2.

Team Wish List supports team members in making requests of each other to establish how they will best work together.

Yin/Yang Analysis: Examining Productive and Counterproductive Traits engages team members in identifying and presenting the productive and counterproductive traits of the team, based upon use of the MBTI, Keirsey Temperament Sorter, or some other personality profile.

What to Keep in Mind When Facilitating These Learning Activities

- Generate excitement, acceptance, and expectation for participation.
- Create relationship.
- Initiate the team to create belonging, trust, and orientation within the team.

Learning Goal

To provide an Initiating experience promoting communication and relationship among team members by having them tell their stories—visually expressing their uniqueness as persons and as team members.

Preparation

1. Photocopy the Personal Mandala handout for all participants.
2. Tear off sheets of flip chart paper for each participant and place them in an out-of-the-way place.
3. Tear off two-inch strips of masking tape and place the tape on the walls of the room, two strips for each participant, in groups of four to six.
4. Provide enough magic markers for each participant to have access to four or more colors.

Learning Activity

1. Begin by explaining that a mandala is a visual representation of prized values, beliefs, and viewpoints held by individuals and groups that captures their essence or "spirit." Mandala is the Sanskrit world for "circle." These art forms are particularly common in the East, especially in India.
2. Provide participants with sheets of flip chart paper and a variety of colored markers.
3. Distribute the Personal Mandala handout. Review the four quadrants with participants:

• Source of personal pride (something the participant is especially proud of in any realm of personal or work life);

- Gift I bring to the team (a personal strength or capacity that the team member routinely exhibits in work in teams);
- Source of frustration with the team (an irritation or upset that the team member experiences or has experienced with this team or other teams);
- Team spirit goal (an intention that the participant has for the team in order to become a spirited, high-performing team).

The ribbon displayed at the bottom of the mandala provides space for a personal credo—an essential, guiding principle or perspective that the individual relies on as a guide for everyday life. This may be an inspired thought, the title of a book or a piece of music, a line of poetry, or any belief that the participant is called to, expressed in a phrase or short sentence.

4. Instruct individuals to *use only images, icons, or pictures* that symbolize their responses to each of the four quadrants. The credo, however, is to be completed in written form. Ask participants to put their names at the top of their papers. Allow 15 minutes to complete the mandalas.

5. After the mandalas are completed, assign participants to teams of four to six persons. Designate a separate area of the room for each team. Note the masking tape positioned in each of these areas of the room, and ask participants to tape their mandalas to the wall.

6. Within the small groups, each participant describes what he or she has drawn in each of the four quadrants and responds to questions from the team. Suggest that one member monitor time to give each participant an equal opportunity to share. Allow 10 to 15 minutes, approximately two to three minutes for each team member in the small group.

7. Reassemble the full group. Ask participants to share their individual goals for the workshop and one other quadrant of their choice.

8. Discuss how participant goals relate to the goals of the workshop.

What to Expect

This activity uses a mode of expression that taps into a deeper level of knowing. The response to a request for drawing the elements of the mandala is often a moan or expression of concern about one's artistic ability. Don't attempt to make the activity okay with participants; merely acknowledge their concerns and create momentum to continue the activity, encouraging participants to choose visual images and commit them to paper.

This is a powerful activity that allows the team to learn a great deal about each other in a brief period of time. The sharing of sources of pride and gifts fosters new awareness among team members about their uniqueness. Sharing team frustrations allows team members to express their concerns about the team. Sharing the team spirit goals permits members to identify what the team most needs to do or be to become a spirited team. It is useful to prompt participants after they have created their mandalas to consider that their team frustration is something that operates within; that is, that the frustration is not "out there," but that it operates within themselves. The team spirit goals allow participants the opportunity to declare their hopes for the team at its best, and they often represent a transformation of the frustration that was identified.

Approximate time: 60 minutes.

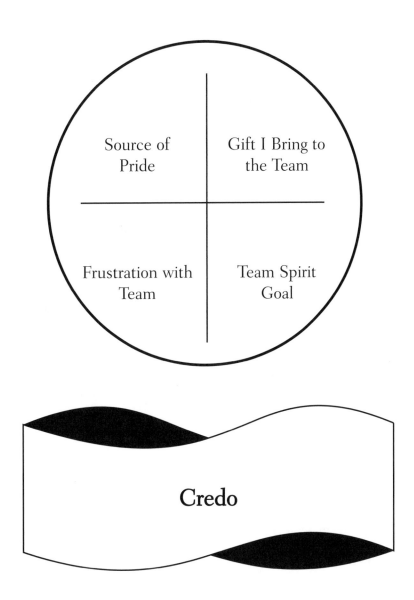

Source of
Pride

Gift I Bring to
the Team

Frustration with
Team

Team Spirit
Goal

Credo

Photocopied from *Building Team Spirit* by Barry Heermann.
Published by McGraw-Hill, ISBN 0-07-028472-5. To order, call 1-800-2MCGRAW.

Learning Goals

1. To promote authentic communication and disclosure among team members about those aspects of their own spirit that they wish to improve by leading them to discern their own movement through the Team Spirit Spiral.
2. To encourage the establishment of coaching relationships between team members that enhance their growth and development along the phases of the Spiral.

Preparation

1. Prepare a lecturette on the use of the Team Spirit Spiral for personal development (see Appendix C, lecturette 2).
2. Photocopy the Operational Levels of Team Spirit handout for all participants.
3. Photocopy the Plotting Possibilities for Individual Growth handout for all participants.

Learning Activity

1. Present a lecturette on the use of the Team Spirit Spiral for personal development as distinct from team development. Distribute the Operational Levels of Team Spirit handout. Emphasize that the Spiral is not only a way to understand the spirit of teams, but it is also a useful way to consider the dynamics of whole organizations, interpersonal relationships, *and* personal development. Review the phases of the Spiral, noting the intrapersonal implications and using yourself as an example. For example, on celebrating relationships you might say, "I sense in my

own life that I don't always appreciate how satisfying my relationships are with my family and work associates."

2. Distribute the Plotting Possibilities for Individual Growth in Spirit handout to all team members, and instruct participants to indicate in the space provided the phase of the Spiral that they would most like to develop more fully in their lives and work relationships. (Note that for most persons there occurs a pattern that cuts across all dimensions of living, whether in the family or at work.) Allow three minutes.

3. Ask the team to assemble into triads and share those phases of the Spiral that they wish to enhance in their lives, and especially in their relationships with the team. Ask each participant to explain how that quality manifests itself in his or her daily life. Allow 15 minutes for sharing, 5 minutes per person. Suggest that within the five minutes participants ask for feedback and assistance from the members of their triad.

4. Request that team members now pair up with another member. When pairs have been formed, ask that they establish a coaching relationship wherein each partner discloses issues that are related to his or her most important phase of team spirit and how he or she is currently inhibited in developing that quality. Request that each participant ask for coaching. Request that the coaching partners meet once a week for a half hour to report on how they are doing, establishing a schedule of meetings for the next month. Coaches should support their partners in taking initiatives that will help them develop the team spirit quality they want, creating concrete goals and projects that will support them in the intervening period. Allow 15 minutes for this conversation in coaching pairs.

5. Complete this activity by asking the team to come back together. Ask the participants to share what they have learned from this activity.

6. Propose a meeting session that will occur in one month so that coaching partners can report on their progress.

What to Expect

Make sure participants are clear about what is meant by the intrapersonal dimension of team spirit (i.e., that the Spiral is operating within individuals as well as teams). This activity is particularly valuable to help participants identify the most important quality of team spirit in their personal and work lives. It also helps to clarify the value structure that is integral to team spirit. Reinforce the fact that team spirit is present in our personal as well as our work lives.

Approximate time: 60 minutes.

community

organization

team and group

interpersonal

intrapersonal

1. Reflect on the movements of the Spiral in your own life, in your relationships with your family and friends, at work, and in all aspects of your day-to-day affairs. Look for a particular phase of the Spiral that pinpoints an area that you might wish to develop more fully. Record your response in the space below.

SERVICE

LETTING GO

CELEBRATING

CLAIMING

VISIONING

INITIATING

TEAM SPIRIT SPIRAL

2. The phase of the Spiral that I would most like to develop in my life and work relationships is:_____

Photocopied from *Building Team Spirit* by Barry Heermann.
Published by McGraw-Hill, ISBN 0-07-028472-5. To order, call 1-800-2MCGRAW.

Learning Goals

1. To help team members appreciate the diversity of their membership, noticing the diversity represented and missing on the team.
2. To support the team members to openly share their experiences and to celebrate the uniqueness and differences of team members.

Preparation

1. Arrange for a large, open space free of tables and chairs.

Learning Activity

1. Ask the team to stand together as a group at one end of the room. You should position yourself with the group at the same end of the room.
2. Explain that the first part of this learning activity will be done in silence and that participants will remain standing during this portion of the experience. Tell participants they will walk to the opposite end of the room each time you call out a category of difference that "fits" or describes who they are. Assure team members that they can elect not to walk to the other end of the room when you identify differences they would prefer not to acknowledge to the group.
3. Coach the team that they should notice who is with them and who is separated from them for each area of difference, noticing the quality of spirit and how they feel about all differences that are mentioned in the learning activity (i.e., when they are present with the group and when they are separated from the group).
4. As an area of difference is identified that "fits" with team members, they should walk to the other end of the room, turn to those members who

walked with them, and silently make eye contact with each member. These persons should then look back at their colleagues, observing their own feelings, before returning back to the full team. (Note: As the facilitator you should walk to the other end of the room for all differences that apply to you, too. Also, it is important that you remain value-neutral and refrain from sharing or acknowledging persons in any category.)

5. Request that all participants maintain the confidentiality of their colleagues during this activity. Achieve agreement on this ground rule from all team participants.

6. For each area of difference the facilitator provides the following instructions:

   Please walk to the other side of the room if you are (name the category of difference).

   Notice who is with you, and silently make eye contact with them.

   Notice who is not with you, looking back at your colleagues.

   Notice the quality of spirit that you feel.

   Please walk back to the full team.

7. The categories of difference are as follows.

   Please walk to the other side of the room if ...

   You are wearing the color red.

   You are a TV fanatic.

   You have brown eyes.

   You have a parent who was a major influence on you.

   You love being in nature.

   You are a vegetarian.

   You are an artist or performer.

   You play a musical instrument.

   You currently have a passion in your life.

   You occasionally feel sad.

   You are a Native American or at least one of your parents is a Native American.

   You are African American or of African descent.

   You are Asian-American or Asian.

   You are Latin American.

   You are of mixed ancestry.

You are a woman.

You have worked for the company for ten years or more.

You are of Jewish background.

You are over 45 years of age.

You are under 25 years of age.

You were raised in a family that was considered poor.

You were raised by a relative other than a parent, or lived in an orphanage or foster home, for some part of your childhood.

You have worked for the company for 20 years or more.

You have lost a brother, sister, mother, or father due to illness.

You were raised by a single parent or currently are a single parent.

You have a family member who is lesbian, gay, or bisexual.

You were raised in a farming community.

You were raised in the Protestant faith.

You have been dangerously sick.

You come from a family in which alcohol or drugs were or are a problem.

You were raised in the Catholic faith.

You or a member of your family has been considered mentally ill.

You were considered fat at any time in your life.

You were not fully able to experience your childhood as circumstances required that you act as an adult.

8. Ask participants what they have learned from this activity. Ask participants to identify how these differences might be leveraged in their work together.

What to Expect

This is a very powerful activity for creating awareness of diversity operating within the team. Don't leave out any parts of the activity. Merely allow the group to savor its diversity, and don't rush the pacing of any part. The strength of the activity is in the silence as members move from one part of the room to the other in response to the categories of differences identified in the activity.

A key component of the activity is the closing part, when participants reflect on the implications of what they experienced. Be aware that some participants may have felt embarrassment or other discomfort during the activity. Encourage team members to express all of their reactions, discerning shifts in their spirit when they walked as well as when they didn't walk. This activity provides a wonderful opportunity for intimate discussions regarding the uniqueness of team members. The key to facilitating this activity successfully is to allow team members to express exactly how they felt, leaving the team with an appreciation of the value of their diversity.

Approximate time: 60-90 minutes.

Learning Goal

To foster deeper relationships among team members through storytelling about their life journeys and the paths that led them to this team.

Preparation

Make several photocopies of the Personal Pathways Timeline Worksheet for each participant.

Learning Activity

1. Explain that at the heart of spirited teams are spirited individuals, and that the purpose of this learning activity is to reveal the unique spirit of each person in the team through storytelling. Clarify that for the first part of the activity each member of the team will work alone to identify the major pathways that characterize his or her individual story.

2. Instruct team members to relax, letting go of the immediate challenges that they face. Ask team members to reflect on their lives in five-year segments, beginning at birth to age five, continuing from age six to ten, and so on, through their current age. Distribute the Personal Pathways Timeline Worksheets to all participants. Note that the worksheet is divided into five-year segments.

3. Using this worksheet, ask participants to write about the critical circumstances of their lives, the major turning points, the pathways taken and not taken, how they felt during those times, and how they feel about them today. When completed, ask participants to name their overall stories as they would a title of a book, a movie, or a song. They will have 20 minutes to work alone, recollecting experiences for each of the five-year segments on the handout provided.

4. After 20 minutes, ask the team if they require more time to complete their worksheets. Allow additional time if necessary. Ask participants to reflect back on all of the pathways and undercurrents that represent their lives, and place a check mark next to those events and situations that most significantly shaped their spirits.

5. Have the team assemble into groups of three or four, sharing the stories of their individual pathways. Ask that each participant elaborate on those pathways that most influenced his or her spirit. Allow four minutes per person.

6. After the small-group sharing, ask that each person in the team be introduced by a colleague from the small group, using the stories of their individual pathways. Allow two minutes per introduction, and an additional minute for the team member being introduced to clarify the information. (A 10-member team would require 30-40 minutes for this phase.)

7. After all team members have been introduced and all of the stories have been told, ask the team what they observed about themselves, about their colleagues, and about the team as a result of this learning activity.

What to Expect

This activity provides an opportunity for team members to explore and tell their stories from the perspective of critical junctures in their lives. Team members like to tell their stories, and the team benefits from a heightened awareness of the uniqueness of each team member. The facilitator helps team members to embrace their uniqueness, creating the climate for enhanced team relationships.

Approximate time: 60-90 minutes.

Personal Pathways Timeline Worksheet

Timelines:

Age 1 to 5

_____

_____

Age 6 to 10

_____

_____

Age 11 to 15

_____

_____

Age 16 to 20

_____

_____

Age 21 to 25

_____

_____

Age 26 to 30

_____

_____

Age 31 to 35

_____

_____

Age 36 to 40

_____

_____

Age 41 to 45

_____

_____

Age 46 to 50

_____

_____

Age 51 to 55

_____

_____

Age 56 to 60

_____

_____

Age 61 to 65

_____

_____

Age 66 to 70

_____

_____

Age 71 to 75

_____

_____

Age 76 to 80

_____

_____

Name of your story:

_____

MOUNTAINTOP STORIES

Learning Goals

1. To quickly build connection and relationship among team participants.
2. To achieve a deeper level of understanding of what is important to team participants, providing a context for greater authenticity in their sharing.

Preparation

Photocopy the Five Questions handout for all participants.

Learning Activity

1. Ask participants to reflect on "mountaintop stories" that have occurred throughout their lives—special times when they experienced the grandeur of life at a high level. Provide all participants with the Five Questions handout. Ask the participants to consider the questions on the handout and briefly record immediate impressions for all five questions. Allow five to ten minutes for this work.

2. Instruct the team to form groups of three. Tell them that they will have 12 minutes to share their responses. Explain that the purpose of this learning activity is to engage in storytelling about ourselves so as to come to know each other at a deeper level. The stories should be "mountaintop stories" (moments and times of great accomplishment and spirit). Request that participants take a few minutes to reflect on their responses before beginning the learning activity. Allow two minutes for reflection, and then begin the 12 minutes. This provides four minutes for each person in the triad. Announce when 30 seconds remain in each four-minute period, rotating through the second and third rounds of sharing.

3. At the completion of this time, ask participants to share how they are feeling, what they notice about themselves, what they observe about

their relationships. Engage the team in a conversation about what is required to foster belonging and trust in a team. Ask the team what this suggests that we might do in the future to nurture greater connection. To the extent that a common factor is generated from the group about how they might proceed to foster trust and connection, ask if there is one person in the team who would be willing to be the spirit keeper, responsible for returning the group to this question on a periodic basis.

What to Expect

This activity focuses on the extraordinary events in the lives of participants, and generates high levels of energy among participants. Most participants have not reflected in such depth on those momentous events in their lives. This lively activity heightens awareness among participants about their shared experiences of wonder and awe, creating connections and building relationships. The heightened energy of participants underscores and enhances the impact of the activity.

Approximate time: 45 minutes.

Team Member Handout

Five Questions

1. What are the five most wonderful moments—moments full of spirit—that you can recall in your life?

_____
_____
_____
_____
_____

2. What is the most satisfying thing that you ever made happen?

_____
_____
_____

3. What is the thing that you like to do that gives you the most joy?

_____
_____
_____

4. What person had the greatest impact on your life?

_____

5. What is the greatest moment in the last 100 years for all of humankind and why?

_____
_____
_____
_____
_____
_____
_____
_____
_____
_____
_____
_____
_____
_____

Photocopied from _Building Team Spirit_ by Barry Heermann.
Published by McGraw-Hill, ISBN 0-07-028472-5. To order, call 1-800-2MCGRAW.

PLAY YOUR OWN KIND OF MUSIC

Learning Goals

1. To assist the team in defining its core values using the structure of harmonics presented in Chapter 2.
2. To help the team design the actions needed to support these core values.

Preparation

1. Photocopy the Team Spirit Harmonics handout for all participants.
2. Photocopy the Fill-in-the-Blank handout for all participants.
3. Create seven flip chart displays with the following headings:

> The Dissonant Factor We Are Most Unconscious About
>
> The Dissonant Factor That Most Limits Our Effectiveness
>
> The Consonant Factor Most Honored and Revered by the Team
>
> The Consonant Factor That I Would Most Like from My Colleagues
>
> The Consonant Factor That Would Transform My Relationship with the Team
>
> Ideas for Moving from Dissonance to Consonance
>
> How to Achieve Consonance

Learning Activity

1. Review with the team the structure of harmonics (i.e., the value structure) presented in Chapter 2.

2. Provide all participants with the Fill-in-the-Blank handout. Provide five minutes for team members to work alone to respond to the fill-in-the-blank items.

3. After completing the fill-in-the-blank items, ask the participants to share their responses to each item. Record responses on the flip chart displays you prepared. Work for consensus as to the most critical consonances and dissonances for the first four factors, validating each consonant or dissonant factor that is offered. For the fifth and final factor, ask individual team members to share briefly why this consonant factor is so critical. Record each individual's name next to the factor he or she identifies.

4. For the first and second (dissonant) factors, lead the group in brainstorming half a dozen ways that they could move from dissonance to consonance. Record their responses on the flip chart you prepared.

5. For the third and fourth (consonant) items, ask the group what would have to happen to realize each consonant factor. Record their responses on the flip chart you prepared.

6. For the fifth (consonant) factor, ask the full team to share insights and awareness about their colleagues in terms of this last factor.

What to Expect

Participants reveal a great deal about the team and about themselves in this activity. It is important to reach consensus on the five dimensions in this activity. The process of reaching consensus is as valuable as the result. Be sure to acknowledge those consonant or dissonant factors that were not consensus items.

Approximate time: 60-90 minutes.

Team Member Handout

Fill-in-the-Blank

1. The dissonant factor that I believe we are most unconscious about as a team is:_____.

2. The dissonant factor that I believe most limits our effectiveness is:_____.

3. The consonant factor that I would most like to see honored and revered in my team is:_____.

4. The consonant factor that I would most like my colleagues to display in their relationship to me is:_____.

5. The consonant factor that would transform my relationship to the team is:_____.

Learning Goals

1. To provide an opportunity for team members to discuss what they need from the team to ensure high performance.
2. To encourage personal pledges from each team member to help achieve their wish for the team.

Preparation

1. Create a flip chart display with the heading, Wish List.
2. Provide notepaper for all participants.
3. Tear off sheets of flip chart paper for each participant and place them in an out-of-the-way place.
4. Tear off two-inch strips of masking tape and place the tape on the walls around the room for use by each participant.
5. Provide a dark-colored magic marker for each participant.

Learning Activity

1. Ask team members to consider what they need to maximize the team's work together regarding relationships, goals, roles, procedures, etc.
2. Encourage participants to disclose everything that is important to them, framing their "wish list" in clear statements on the notepaper provided. Allow five minutes, and then ask the participants to share their wish lists. Record all responses on flip chart paper.
3. After recording all the wishes, ask the team to identify patterns in their responses, and then ask the team to prioritize key wishes.

4. Following this activity provide each team member with a sheet of flip chart paper. Direct them to write down "What I am willing to pledge to the team to make our wishes come true."

5. Tape the flip chart papers with their pledges on the wall. Ask each team member to present his or her pledge.

6. After all pledges are presented, ask the team to share their insights and awareness.

What to Expect

Participants in this activity are afforded the opportunity to ask for what they want. This can be a very powerful experience, and all team members feel empowered by making and responding to such requests of the team. Team members also like to give to the team, and this activity provides the opportunity to pledge precisely the gift that each one wants to make available to colleagues. Occasionally team members may decline requests made by other team members; reinforce the idea that this is entirely appropriate. A good request carries no expectation for a particular response.

Approximate time: 60-90 minutes.

YIN/YANG ANALYSIS: EXAMINING PRODUCTIVE AND COUNTERPRODUCTIVE TRAITS

Learning Goals

1. To provide an opportunity for team members to better understand themselves and their team colleagues through the use of the Keirsey Temperament Sorter, the MBTI, or some other personality inventory.
2. To encourage feedback among team members to enhance team effectiveness.

Preparation

1. Create a flip chart display of a Yin/Yang symbol and post it centrally in the room.
2. Prepare a lecturette on the temperament or personality types encompassed by the Keirsey Temperament Sorter, the MBTI, or other personality inventory for each participant's type.
3. Provide an interpretive report for the personality inventory that is used, whether the Keirsey Temperament Sorter, the MBTI, or another personality inventory for each participant's type.
4. Tear off sheets of flip chart paper for each participant and place in an out-of-the-way place.
5. Tear off two-inch strips of masking tape and place the tape on the walls of the room, two strips for each participant in groups of four to six.
6. Provide a dark-colored magic marker for each participant.

Learning Activity

1. Emphasize that the usefulness of personality inventories is in coming to understand the uniqueness of team members. The major personality inventories stress that there are no good or bad personality types. All personality types are valuable, and the greater the diversity of types present on the team the richer the potential of the team. The purpose of this activity is to enhance appreciation of differences in the team, providing feedback opportunities for team members to discuss those differences. The process of sharing one's productive and counterproductive traits contributes to Initiating, and enables the team to lay the groundwork for becoming a spirited, high-performing team.

2. Provide a lecturette on the temperament or personality types encompassed by the Keirsey Temperament Sorter, the MBTI*, or other personality inventory that is used. (If selecting the Keirsey Temperament Sorter, draw your lecturette from the book *Please Understand Me* by Keirsey and Bates.) Administer the personality inventory selected. Provide interpretive information on the type of each team member as well as the team type (i.e., the combined type of all team members). Ask the team to form dyads, and allow 10 minutes for discussion of individual types.

3. Have the participants review the interpretive information provided from the Keirsey Temperament Sorter or other personality inventory. Instruct them to underline key phrases that accurately describe their tendencies and temperament. Have them place a 1 next to those phrases that indicate a productive trait and a 2 next to those that indicate a counterproductive trait. In addition, encourage the participants to reflect on all their experiences with their team and record any additional traits of theirs that may not have shown up in the personality inventory. Allow ten minutes.

4. Provide each participant with a piece of flip chart paper. Post the flip chart display of the Yin/Yang symbol and ask participants to reproduce it. Ask the team if anyone is familiar with the meaning of this ancient Chinese symbol. (Explain that the Yin/Yang represents the forces of light and dark, male and female, positive and negative, good and evil, etc., that exist within all things.) Direct participants to record their productive traits on one side of the symbol and their counterproductive traits on the opposite side of the symbol. Ask participants to write their names on the top of their flip chart papers.

*Please be aware that a certification program is required for facilitating the MBTI.

5. Organize team members into subgroups of four to six. Designate areas of the room for each subgroup and direct participants to post their symbols on the wall in their assigned area with the masking tape.

6. Ask the group to designate an initial focus person. This person will have five minutes to present his or her Yin/Yang symbol illustrating the productive and counterproductive traits *and* to receive feedback from peers on the team. Within the five minutes and after the presentation by the focus person, the feedback persons acknowledge, add to, discuss, and provide constructive feedback to the focus person.

   (Note: See Chapter 7, Letting Go through Constructive Feedback as a possible adjunct to this activity.)

7. At the end of the first five-minute round, another member of the subgroup rotates into the focus person role, presents his or her Yin/Yang analysis, and receives feedback from colleagues for five minutes. This rotation continues until all have served as focus persons.

8. When all participants have presented their Yin/Yang analyses to their subgroups, reconvene the full team for a discussion of the experience. Ask participants what they learned about themselves and their colleagues that will be helpful in working together as a team.

What to Expect

This activity provides participants honest, clear feedback about their productive and counterproductive traits. Because of the attention to the dark as well as the light side of each team member, it provides a striking opportunity to speak openly and forthrightly. It is important to control time allotments for the exercise. Should some tension between team members arise from this activity, suggest that those persons continue to work through their communications at another time if the time provided isn't sufficient for adequate closure. Assure the participants that upcoming sessions will provide explicit opportunities to continue to engage in more open and forthright conversation.

Approximate time: 60-90 minutes.

4

Visioning the Future

Not much happens without a dream.
And for something great to happen, there must be a great dream.
Much more than a dreamer is required to bring it to reality;
but the dream must be there first.
Robert Greenleaf

There is a dream dreaming us.
African Bushman

Visioning is the mind's way of conceptualizing a possible reality. Anything ever accomplished began with an idea, a dream, a vision. Visioning inspires teams, calling them forth to a new future. Visions stimulate the senses and have shape. A good vision portrays the destination reached and the goal attained. Visioning focuses on the future and not the present or the past. It is pointed toward some desired end state, not at how to get there. A great vision allows the team to touch its spirit.

Effective facilitation of Visioning supports the team in inquiring into these kinds of questions:

- What should our purpose be?
- What core values do we prize?
- What is it that motivates us?
- What do we do best and how does that relate to the service we provide to customers?
- What kind of future do we want to create?
- How can this team make a difference both in serving customers and to its own membership?

Exemplary facilitation of Visioning allows the team to assert:

The XYZ team is the world leader in ...

The ABC team is the foremost provider of ...

The 123 team is an ultimate developer and deliverer of ...

Spirited, high-performing teams are motivated to make a difference by generously serving customers. This contribution yields financial and other rewards for the team. But the transcendent reward for fulfilling the vision is the sense of awe and wonder and the connectedness that is experienced by the team. These are the manifestations of spirit.

Team members also vision the content and quality of their relationships. Visioning the team's Service to each other is a prime consideration of spirited teams.

There is a spiritual hunger, a longing for meaning and purpose, that is present in individuals, teams, and organizations. Great Visioning responds to these needs of team members and customers. It is only after Visioning rich Service to each other and to customers that teams are able to realize the financial return; it is not the other way around.

The following guidelines for facilitating the team's development of vision and values are designed to foster an environment that encourages Visioning as an ongoing way of thinking and being:

1. Support team members in exploring and developing a rich and vital personal vision for their lives and work. Humans have a primary desire to have a purpose and to follow it passionately. Support for personal Visioning is a cornerstone of great teams: Powerful team visions flow out of and through vital and positive individual visions. The capacity to see possibilities and think expansively in one's personal life is transferable to team Visioning. The activities in this volume engage participants at the levels of both personal vision and team vision, as well as in the integration of personal and team vision.

2. Help the team develop awareness about and understand the necessary conditions for generating a breakthrough. Conventional thinking suggests that change is always incremental and predictable over time. Have the team consider the following graph that distinguishes incremental change from a breakthrough, with time on the horizontal axis and some intended result on the vertical axis (e.g., sales, customer satisfaction, a productivity index).

When facilitating the activities in this volume, request that team members consider the kind of complete reformulation in thinking that would foster a breakthrough, whether predictable or unpredictable. Engender discussion about the context necessary for creating such a breakthrough.

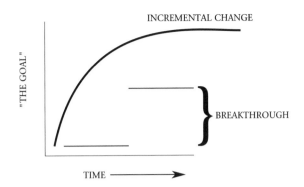

3. Encourage the team to discover a metaphor that frees them to reveal the most extraordinary possibilities. The activities in this volume frequently call up metaphors used in the wider culture, especially the culture of organizations. Metaphors drawn from athletics or war produce shallower and narrower thinking than metaphors from nature or the arts (for example music, the change in seasons, theater, or healing).

4. Encourage the team to express its vision in symbolic and graphic forms. Using symbolic visual forms allows the team to tap into a very different dimension. It enables them to step outside of existing paradigms.

5. Encourage the team to distill out of its Visioning a vision statement or credo (a phrase or sentence at most), as well as a fuller expression of the vision in the form of a mission statement (typically a paragraph that clarifies the strategic intent of the team and the team's core values). These vision statements or credos may be developed out of conversation or they may emerge out of work in symbolic and visual realms.

6. Visioning moves the team into the next phase of the Spiral, Claiming. Therefore, beyond facilitating the team to reveal its most vital and enlivening image of Service (the team's intended end state), it is important to help the team to identify where it is now, so it can construct an action plan to realize the vision. Helping the team to be clear about this discrepancy between where the team is and where it wants to go uncovers creative tension and clarifies the path to the vision. Because the world does not necessarily cooperate with the realization of vision, a plan that supports the achievement of the vision is important. Such a plan is best conceived by working backward from the vision, defining desired results, milestones, and the path the team needs to take. Facilitate the team's process of developing a plan that addresses requisite skills, support structures, and systems.

When facilitating the activities in this volume, emphasize that Visioning is not just an event completed as part of a team spirit learning activity. It is a starting point. Visioning is an ongoing process of thinking and being that pervades the work of the team. The learning activities in this chapter help teams to reveal and realize their vision of extraordinary team performance and to create awareness about this ongoing process.

The Learning Activities

Creating a Personal Vision: Dialogue with a Wisdom Figure focuses on the development of individual visions.

Fostering Consonant Values to Achieve Extraordinary Team Relationships assists the team in clarifying and identifying its critical values.

Celebrating Where We Are and Going Beyond supports the team in acknowledging and building upon its strengths to create a further improvement in effectiveness.

Achieving a Spirit Leap in Enhancing Customer Service focuses externally on visions of how to serve customers best.

Team Mandala integrates considerations of serving the team and customers using visual and symbolic forms.

Team Obituary: Reflecting on the End to Create the Future asks the team to consider its demise as a way of clarifying its future.

A Values Activity: Rites of Passage requests that the team focus on its life phases to better understand its key values.

Flight of Fancy engages the team in a high-altitude view of the team in the next decade.

Note: Review the learning activities for Service in Chapter 9, as they can be used to further clarify team vision and values.

What to Keep in Mind When Facilitating These Learning Activities

- Create possibility for team members and the team so that they can come to discover their most vibrant visions.
- Be present to and share the unique spirit of Service that you perceive is operating within the team.
- Support the team in its efforts to reveal its own destiny and soul.

CREATING A PERSONAL VISION: DIALOGUE WITH A WISDOM FIGURE

Learning Goals

1. To promote awareness in the team of the importance of individual vision.
2. To prompt new thinking about what each member wants in the future.

Preparation

1. Provide notepaper for all participants.
2. Photocopy the Key Life Questions handout for all participants.
3. Photocopy the Wisdom Figure Dialogue Questions handout for all participants.

Learning Activity

1. Explain that team Visioning occurs best when team members have developed their own vibrant personal visions. Teams whose members are excited about their individual futures are more vital and resourceful than teams whose members feel stuck or are unclear in their life purposes. Assure participants that they will have complete anonymity in this activity and will share only what they choose to share with their colleagues.

2. Request that team members work alone to focus on unearthing and discovering those future scenarios that call to them. Emphasize that vocation is an inner knowing or calling forth of our energies and resources to serve others. The secret is in listening to that inner knowing.

3. Suggest that participants release the tensions of the day, relax, breathe deeply, and listen to their inner voices. From this place of quiet, ask team members to reflect on all of those persons in their lives who have served as a source of wisdom and inspiration to them. When ready, ask participants to make a list of these wisdom figures on the notepaper provided. Allow five minutes for this individual work.

4. Ask team members to select one person who has served as the greatest source of wisdom for them. When all team members have selected wisdom figures, ask participants to turn to the person sitting next to them,

describe the wisdom figure they chose, and explain why they selected that person. Allow five minutes for this activity.

5. In preparation for a dialogue with the wisdom figures, have the participants respond to a series of life-probing questions. Distribute the Key Life Questions handout. Allow 10 to 15 minutes for team members to record their responses.

6. Explain that before team members can meaningfully begin dialogues with their wisdom figures you have a question that you would like to pose, and ask: "Are you willing to have a breakthrough in your lives? Such a breakthrough will require that you take full responsibility for shifting your obstacles into projects. Are you willing to do that?"

7. Direct participants to enter into imaginary dialogue with their wisdom figures in a series of questions. Distribute the Wisdom Figure Dialogue Questions handout. Explain that the handout provided is divided into two columns, one for their questions and observations in response to the wisdom figure and one for the wisdom figure's responses and observations. Allow 10 to 20 minutes for team members to record their responses.

8. When all team members have responded to all questions and have completed their dialogue with their wisdom figures, ask for sharing. What did participants observe as they completed the various phases of the exercise? What do they notice about themselves? About their futures? About the obstacles that they face?

What to Expect

This activity helps team members to explore their dreams and ambitions. Because some of those dreams and ambitions may be outside the boundaries of the team's charter, some team members will be reticent to share the results of this activity with the team or team leader. Reinforce the fact that while participants can have complete anonymity in this activity, they are encouraged to share their insights as that sharing will further empower them to realize their intentions.

This activity is a useful prelude to a Visioning activity focused on team vision and values. To aid in the transition from individual to team vision, it is helpful to have team members discuss the process that helped them reveal their personal vision and its relationship to the process for revealing potent team vision. Similarly, engage participants in consideration of how their personal visions "fit" their team visions. Encourage those team members whose visions are seemingly divergent from the team vision to reconcile those differences, clarifying how their current participation on the team is a stepping-stone to the future.

Approximate time: 60-90 minutes.

Key Life Questions

a. What is the greatest source of passion in your life?

_____

_____

_____

_____

_____

_____

b. What is it that you do that gives you the most pleasure?

_____

_____

_____

_____

_____

_____

c. What do you most enjoy doing avocationally? Vocationally?

_____

_____

_____

_____

_____

_____

d. What are the major transitions that you have made or contemplated making in your life?

_____

_____

_____

_____

_____

_____

Photocopied from _Building Team Spirit_ by Barry Heermann.
Published by McGraw-Hill, ISBN 0-07-028472-5. To order, call 1-800-2MCGRAW.

e. If you could do anything that you wished in the world, what would that one thing be?

_____

_____

_____

_____

_____

_____

f. Where would you like to be in five years?

_____

_____

_____

_____

_____

_____

g. What are the obstacles in the way of your achieving your five-year vision?

_____

_____

_____

_____

_____

_____

Wisdom Figure Dialogue Questions

Respond to each of the following questions, taking approximately three to five minutes per question, providing observations and reactions for yourself and for the wisdom figure.

You: **Wisdom Figure:**_____

What resources do you perceive   _____
that I have to realize the future   _____
that I want to create for myself?   _____
                                              _____
                                              _____
                                              _____
                                              _____
                                              _____

What coaching do you have for   _____
me, given your knowledge of me   _____
and sensitivity to my strengths   _____
and counterproductive traits?   _____
                                              _____
                                              _____
                                              _____

Do you believe that what I am   _____
doing now is helpful for   _____
building the kind of future   _____
I want?   _____
                                              _____
                                              _____
                                              _____

You: **Wisdom Figure:**_____

How can my current work on
the team help me to achieve the
future I am creating?

_____
_____
_____
_____
_____
_____
_____
_____

Who do you believe I should
consult about the future that
I want to create?

_____
_____
_____
_____
_____
_____
_____
_____

What do you perceive to be my
greatest inner strength that I
can draw upon to move to the
future that I want?

_____
_____
_____
_____
_____
_____
_____
_____

What should I do right now
to accomplish the future
I want? And then what?...
And then what?...And then
what?   And then what?

_____
_____
_____
_____
_____
_____
_____
_____

Photocopied from *Building Team Spirit* by Barry Heermann.
Published by McGraw-Hill, ISBN 0-07-028472-5. To order, call 1-800-2MCGRAW.

Learning Goal

To vision and prioritize those values that lead to extraordinary team relationships and identify the actions necessary to support those values in the team.

Preparation

1. Photocopy the Team Spirit Harmonics handout for all participants.
2. Provide notepaper for all participants.
3. Create a flip chart display of stairs with eight separate steps.
4. Create a flip chart display with the heading, Strategies to Create Greater Consonance in Our Team.

Learning Activity

1. Tell participants you would like them to identify those consonant values that are most important to supporting their vision of the very highest quality team relationships. Distribute the Team Spirit Harmonics handout. Ask participants to individually review the Team Spirit Consonances, select the five most important consonant values for the team to develop, and rank them in order of importance on the notepaper provided. Allow five to ten minutes for individual work.
2. Present the flip chart display of stairs with eight separate steps.
3. Help the team achieve consensus on their eight preferred consonances, delineating a pattern of values that the team visions for its work together. Next, reach consensus on the ranking of these consonances. Lead a discussion with the team about its ranking and the rationale behind that ranking. Record their consensus ranking on the flip chart display

4. Request that the team work quietly in triads to identify strategies for developing these values in the team. Provide ten minutes for work in triads.

5. Request that the team return as a full group, and ask the triads to share strategies that the team can implement to achieve the desired level of consonance. Reach consensus on the preferred strategies and record them on the flip chart display you have prepared.

6. Lead a discussion with the team about how embracing these consonant values would contribute to a deepening of the team's relationships and to an improvement of team results. In closing, ask members to share their observations and thinking as a result of participating in this activity.

What to Expect:

Team participants have different needs and expectations. This activity will be beneficial to the extent that all participants share their ideas on what consonant values are most important to team functioning and why. Encourage full participation and take the time to achieve consensus among team members. Establish agreement among team members about how they will proceed to create such consonance, using concrete strategies.

Approximate time: 60-75 minutes.

CONSONANCES

(a combination of musical tones that have resolved—that is, they are in agreement)

Service
-*contribution*: generously and freely giving to another
-*aligned execution*: fulfilling, in a unified way, customer and team needs
-*mutual support*: providing reciprocal assistance

Initiating
-*orientation*: becoming familiarized and aware
-*belonging*: feeling allied with and a part of the team
-*trust*: feeling reliant and secure about team members

Visioning
-*shared vision/values*: agreeing on what is possible and its underlying worth and merit
-*compassion*: experiencing empathy and concern for another
-*presence*: deeply experiencing the purpose of the team

Claiming
-*goal/role alignment*: agreeing on the outcome and the means for achieving it
-*organization support*: securing the necessary resources from the organization
-*competence*: developing skills and awareness needed to perform team roles

Celebrating
-*appreciation*: feeling recognized and acknowledged
-*energy*: experiencing vitality and aliveness
-*wonder*: experiencing an unbounded sense of possibility

Letting Go
-*disclosure*: revealing previously suppressed attitudes and opinions
-*constructive feedback*: providing forthright responses that encourage growth
—*completion*: feeling a sense of freedom when everything has been said

DISSONANCES

(a combination of unresolved musical tones)

Service
-*depletion*: feeling used up, unable to freely give to another
-*uncoordinated action*: incompletely fulfilling customer and team needs
-*unsupportiveness*: acting without concern for others

Initiating
-*disorientation*: experiencing disequilibrium and fear
-*alienation*: feeling like a misfit, not a part of the team
-*mistrust*: feeling insecure and cautious about team members

Visioning
-*ambiguous vision/values*: experiencing uncertainty about what is possible—let alone its underlying worth and merit
-*callousness*: being insensitive and harsh
-*aridness*: feeling barren and empty, without a sense of purpose

Claiming
-*nonalignment*: disagreeing about the outcome and means for achieving it
-*nonsupport*: being unable to secure the necessary resources from the organization
-*deficiency*: not having the skills and awareness needed to perform team roles

Celebrating
-*nonappreciation*: not feeling recognized and acknowledged
-*burnout*: feeling used up and ineffective in the team
-*disenchantment*: feeling repelled and put out

Letting Go
-*withheld communication*: concealing attitudes and opinions from others
-*criticism*: offering unsupportive critical feedback
-*incompletion*: feeling regretful about withholding communications

Photocopied from *Building Team Spirit* by Barry Heermann.
Published by McGraw-Hill, ISBN 0-07-028472-5. To order, call 1-800-2MCGRAW.

ACTIVITY
CELEBRATING WHERE WE ARE
AND GOING BEYOND

Learning Goals

1. To identify an area in which the team currently exhibits high levels of spirit.
2. To visualize a breakthrough in spirit that the team can generate in this area and specify concrete actions for achieving the breakthrough in spirit.

Preparation

1. Provide notepaper for all participants.
2. Create three flip chart displays with the headings:

   Areas of High Spiritedness in This Team

   Potential Breakthrough in Spirit

   What We Need to Do to Create a Breakthrough in Spirit

Learning Activity

1. Ask the team to brainstorm those aspects of their current work together that are most spirit-filled (e.g., identifying those areas where they are most masterful, where they most experience the joy of their work together, where there is greatest synergy, power, and delight). Record their responses on the flip chart you have prepared, creating a heightened awareness of the spiritedness in the team.* Help the team to identify the one or two areas of greatest team spiritedness.

---

*See Chapter 6, Fostering Celebration: An Interview and Discussion Process, as a potential prelude to this learning activity. The Chapter 6 activity generates considerable data about the team's greatness, setting the stage for this activity.

2. Based upon the team's identification of the areas where it exhibits the greatest spirit, explain that you would now like individual team participants to consider what a breakthrough beyond this would look like. Ask team members to individually generate responses on notepaper to the following question (allow about five minutes):

What would this breakthrough in spirit look like in terms of the quality of team relationships, the team's performance and results produced, and the regard for the team demonstrated by its organization, industry or sector of service, and customers?

3. When all team members have completed their responses, request that they share their thoughts. Record their responses regarding a potential breakthrough in spirit on the flip chart you have prepared.

4. After recording their responses, ask the team to choose the two or three most exciting and enlivening breakthroughs in the spirit of the team.

5. Request that the team work in triads to develop action steps to create the environment for such a breakthrough in spirit. Ask the triads to consider what the team would have to do and how it would have to be to support such a breakthrough in spirit. Allow ten minutes.

6. Ask the triads to share their action steps with the entire team. Record the ideas on the flip chart you have prepared. Achieve consensus from the team about the next steps they will take to achieve a breakthrough in spirit.

7. Ask the team to share any other thoughts they have as a result of participating in this Visioning activity.

What to Expect

The success of this activity depends on developing awareness of two realities. The first is a concrete example of the team's own greatness and power. Take time for the team to fully savor and celebrate their most spirited work together. The second is the potential for a breakthrough beyond the grandeur of the incident of spirited performance identified previously. Some team members may be unclear about what is meant by a breakthrough. Draw on the introductory material from this chapter, specifically the graphic representation of a breakthrough on page 81, to clarify this idea of a radical shift in performance. Allow the group to explore the implications of a breakthrough without moving on too quickly.

Approximate time: 60-90 minutes.

Learning Goals

1. To create a vision of greatly enhanced customer service.
2. To reach consensus about actions that the team can take to promote this leap to enhanced service.

Preparation

1. Photocopy the Spirit Leap handout for all participants.
2. Create two flip chart displays, labeled Spirit Leap and Action Steps to Achieve a Spirit Leap.

Learning Activity

1. In preparation for this activity, ask the team to identify the primary customer or customers that they serve (internal or external). Allow five minutes for discussion regarding the primary customer(s) for the team's product or service. Explain that shortly the team will respond to questions that will probe what a spirit leap would look like in serving their customer. To accomplish this, the team will consider their current competitive position with key customers. Based upon this exploration of competitors, participants will explore the capabilities and modes of thinking that influence how they serve customers. Distribute the Spirit Leap handout, and ask participants to work on them individually, providing responses that are bold and creative. Allow 10 to 15 minutes for participants to record their responses on the Spirit Leap handout.

2. Ask participants to share what they noticed about themselves as they were completing the handout. Ask them to share their leaps in spirit and

how they perceive these leaps will impact customer service. Record all responses on the flip chart you have prepared.

3. After recording all of the leaps in spirit and related images, request that team members discuss the implications of their responses.

   • Do they discern patterns in their responses?

   • Where do team members notice the most excitement among the ideas generated?

   • Allow time for open discussion around the two or three responses that generate the most enthusiasm.

4. Ask the team to generate five concrete action steps for changing current work procedures or for developing new work procedures to realize one of the spirit leaps. Record their action steps on the flip chart you have prepared. Develop consensus for the best ideas to advance customer service.

5. Conclude by asking the team what they noticed or observed as a result of this exercise.

What to Expect

This activity is designed to move team members beyond their current thinking regarding how they can best serve customers. By responding to the Spirit Leap handout, participants will begin to see new possibilities. The success of this activity hinges on developing clear images of enhanced customer service. Achieving consensus on strategic action steps to accomplish such a shift in service is the pivotal result of this activity.

Approximate time: 60-90 minutes.

Spirit Leap

Provide responses to each of the following questions:

1. Who are our customers today?

   _____
   _____
   _____

2. Who are our customers likely to be in five years?

   _____
   _____
   _____

3. What customer benefits will we be required to deliver five years from now?

   _____
   _____
   _____

4. Who are our competitors?

   _____
   _____
   _____

5. What are our current advantages over our competitors in serving customers?

   _____
   _____
   _____

6. What skills are present in the team that contribute to these advantages?

   _____
   _____
   _____

7. What advantages will we need to create over our competitors to serve customers five years from now?

   _____
   _____
   _____

8. What skills are present in the team that could contribute to the advantages that will be required five years from now?

   _____
   _____
   _____

Photocopied from *Building Team Spirit* by Barry Heermann.
Published by McGraw-Hill, ISBN 0-07-028472-5. To order, call 1-800-2MCGRAW.

9. What other skills will we need to develop or bring onto the team?

_____

_____

10. What are the gaps or niches in and around our existing products or services that we might develop to serve customers better?

_____

_____

11. What rule-breaking path might we take to radically improve our service to customers?

_____

_____

12. Through what channels might we better serve customers?

_____

_____

13. What will a leap in spirit look like concretely in terms of new products or services for customers?

_____

_____

14. How will the team's work together change in order to deliver this new level of Service?

_____

_____

15. What will this leap in spirit mean in terms of funding, physical realities (e.g., facilities), and composition of the team?

_____

_____

16. How will this leap in spirit impact the quality of life of those served?

_____

_____

_____

Photocopied from *Building Team Spirit* by Barry Heermann.
Published by McGraw-Hill, ISBN 0-07-028472-5. To order, call 1-800-2MCGRAW.

Learning Goal:

To clarify the team's vision and values as they relate to serving the team and serving customers, by creating a team mandala.

Preparation:

1. Photocopy the Three Phases of the Team Mandala Activity handout for all participants.
2. Acquire a sufficient number of easels, flip chart tablets, and magic markers to accommodate subteams.
3. Photocopy the Team Spirit Harmonics handout for all participants.

Learning Activity

1. Begin by reviewing the purpose of this activity and its importance to the spirit of the team. Explain that through this activity the team will touch the spirit of the team, making it tangible.
2. Ask participants to form subteams of three to five.
3. Distribute the Three Phases of the Team Mandala Activity handout. Clarify that mandala is Sanskrit for "circle." A mandala, particularly common in the East, visually symbolizes the heartfelt values of a family or group. Ask subteams to create a Team Mandala that is a visual representation of the team's distinctive core values and vision, working through the three phases of the activity as displayed in the handout. Emphasize that each subteam should develop the richest and most expansive vision of the future imaginable for serving customers and serving each other.

4. For the first phase, subteams are to consider what is at the heart of team functioning from the perspective of Service to customers. The subteam should begin by brainstorming what it sees as the essence of the team's work together in serving customers. Ask subteams, "What is the team's reason for being?" A facilitator is appointed to record and ultimately prioritize brainstorming ideas. When brainstorming and prioritization are complete, about halfway through the first phase, the subteams should move to developing a visual form that captures the language identified through brainstorming. Allow approximately 20 to 30 minutes for the completion of this phase of of the exercise.

5. Explain that for the second phase of the exercise, subteams are to consider what is at the heart of team functioning from the perspective of Service to other members of the team. The subteam should begin by brainstorming what they see as the essence of the team's work in supporting and serving each other. Provide the Team Spirit Harmonics handout to stimulate their thinking. A new facilitator is appointed to record and prioritize brainstorming ideas for this phase. When brainstorming is complete, about halfway through this phase, the subteams should move to develop visual forms that capture the language identified through brainstorming. Allow approximately 20 to 30 minutes for the completion of this phase of the exercise.

6. For the third phase of the exercise, subteams are to integrate their visions of the heart of team functioning, from the perspectives of Service to customers and Service to each other. The subteams should consider their brainstorming ideas, focusing particularly on how they can integrate their visual images into one vision or how they might create a totally new visual image that encompasses the two initial images. A new facilitator is appointed for this phase, to bring the team to closure and to develop the visual image. Allow approximately 20 minutes for the completion of the Team Mandala and the third phase of the exercise.

7. After the subteams have completed their work, ask them each to appoint a spokesperson to present their Team Mandala and the thinking that led to the creation of it to the full team. Allow approximately five minutes for each subteam presentation.

8. When all Team Mandalas have been presented, request that one member from each subteam join a task force that will pull together all the ideas presented into a single representation of a unified Team Mandala that the whole team can support. Suggest that the task force might work over an extended lunch break, reporting their recommendations to the

full team after lunch. Alternatively, this learning activity might be offered as an afternoon event, with a recommendation to be presented the next morning.

9. After lunch or the next morning, ask the task force to present its reconceptualized Team Mandala that integrates the ideas and various elements of the subteams' mandalas. Encourage discussion, moving the team to consensus. Allow approximately 20 minutes for discussion.

10. Ask the team members how they would like to display and use their Team Mandala as a reminder of their work together. Ask them what they observed about the Visioning work they undertook.

What to Expect

This is a powerful activity that culminates in the creation of a graphic representation of the essential vision and values of the team. Teams delight in their final product.

When subteams have completed the first two phases of this activity (developing images for customer service and service to the team), there may be some anxiousness about the instruction to integrate the two images of customer and team service. Merely repeat the instruction and encourage subteams to keep looking for ways to integrate their separate visualizations or for some different, third image that combines the essence of the first two images.

After all subteams have created Team Mandalas that integrate all of the elements into one representation and have presented their work to the whole team, it is important to acknowledge the good work of each subteam. Before creating the task force, offer that all of the images provide glimpses into the greatness of this team in its best moments, and that there is some synergistic combination of all these images that will most powerfully represent the spirit of the team. Emphasize that while the task force will support the team's choices for the desired elements of the Team Mandala, it may require some additional discussion in team meetings before agreement is reached on the final representation.

Suggest that the team might seek outside assistance for the final representation of the Team Mandala, e.g., a graphic artist or computer graphics specialist.

Approximate time: 120-150 minutes.

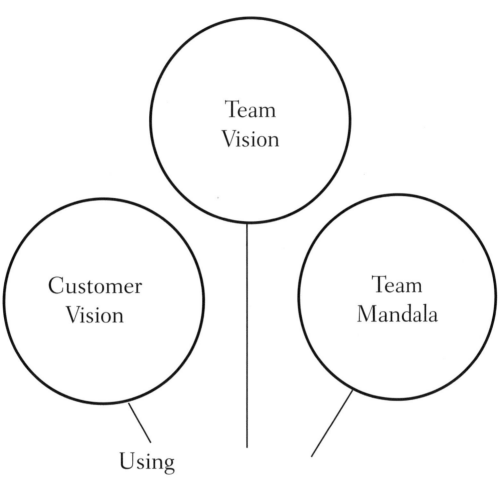

Team
Vision

Customer
Vision

Team
Mandala

Using
1. Language Forms
2. Visual Symbols and Forms

CONSONANCES

(a combination of musical tones that have resolved—that is, they are in agreement)

Service
-contribution: generously and freely giving to another
-aligned execution: fulfilling, in a unified way, customer and team needs
-mutual support: providing reciprocal assistance

Initiating
-orientation: becoming familiarized and aware
-belonging: feeling allied with and a part of the team
-trust: feeling reliant and secure about team members

Visioning
-shared vision/values: agreeing on what is possible and its underlying worth and merit
-compassion: experiencing empathy and concern for another
-presence: deeply experiencing the purpose of the team

Claiming
-goal/role alignment: agreeing on the outcome and the means for achieving it
-organization support: securing the necessary resources from the organization
-competence: developing skills and awareness needed to perform team roles

Celebrating
-appreciation: feeling recognized and acknowledged
-energy: experiencing vitality and aliveness
-wonder: experiencing an unbounded sense of possibility

Letting Go
-disclosure: revealing previously suppressed attitudes and opinions
-constructive feedback: providing forthright responses that encourage growth
—completion: feeling a sense of freedom when everything has been said

DISSONANCES

(a combination of unresolved musical tones)

Service
-depletion: feeling used up, unable to freely give to another
-uncoordinated action: incompletely fulfilling customer and team needs
-unsupportiveness: acting without concern for others

Initiating
-disorientation: experiencing disequilibrium and fear
-alienation: feeling like a misfit, not a part of the team
-mistrust: feeling insecure and cautious about team members

Visioning
-ambiguous vision/values: experiencing uncertainty about what is possible—let alone its underlying worth and merit
-callousness: being insensitive and harsh
-aridness: feeling barren and empty, without a sense of purpose

Claiming
-nonalignment: disagreeing about the outcome and means for achieving it
-nonsupport: being unable to secure the necessary resources from the organization
-deficiency: not having the skills and awareness needed to perform team roles

Celebrating
-nonappreciation: not feeling recognized and acknowledged
-burnout: feeling used up and ineffective in the team
-disenchantment: feeling repelled and put out

Letting Go
-withheld communication: concealing attitudes and opinions from others
-criticism: offering unsupportive critical feedback
-incompletion: feeling regretful about withholding communications

Photocopied from *Building Team Spirit* by Barry Heermann.
Published by McGraw-Hill, ISBN 0-07-028472-5. To order, call 1-800-2MCGRAW.

ACTIVITY
TEAM OBITUARY:
REFLECTING ON THE END TO CREATE THE FUTURE

Learning Goals

1. To clarify team vision and values.
2. To determine next steps in formulating and refining the team's vision and values.

Preparation

1. Photocopy the Team Obituary handout for all participants.
2. Create two flip chart displays with the headings Vision and Values and Action Steps.

Learning Activity

1. Observe that some persons report an unusual clarity of purpose and depth of spirit when faced with a major ending: for example, a serious illness, a death, or a near-death experience. In this learning activity, participants will come face to face with the death of their team in order to become clearer about the critical vision and values that the team embodies. Explain that participants are to project themselves forward in time to the end of the team—which follows abruptly after a period of unusual team resourcefulness and effectiveness. Team members are to write a "glowing" account of the team's unusual success in the form of an obituary for the team.
2. Distribute the Team Obituary handout. Have participants write out their obituaries for the team just as they would like them to appear on the front page of their favorite newspapers. Request that each article include a headline that draws attention to the accomplishments of the team.

Participants will note contributions, accomplishments, and the impact on individual lives attributable to the team by customers, team members, and others touched by the team. Allow 10 to 15 minutes for participants to complete this writing.

3. After completing the obituaries, have volunteers read them. Facilitate a discussion among team members about the insights gleaned from these various obituaries.

4. Request that the team identify and write about the vision and values that will be necessary for the team to embrace in order to achieve the success identified in the obituaries they composed. What steps will the team need to take? Allow five minutes for participants to complete their responses.

5. Ask participants to volunteer elements of their suggested vision and values. Record the responses of team members on the flip chart you have prepared. Ask team members to reach consensus on the most important vision and values they wish to emphasize in their work as a team.

6. Ask the team to generate concrete action steps for putting these values and vision in place. Record the action steps on the flip chart you have prepared, developing consensus on which action steps would best support the accomplishment of these vision and values.

7. Ask participants for any insights or clarification they wish to share as a result of this learning activity.

What to Expect

This activity hinges on developing within the team a heightened sense of their potential greatness. It is important to reinforce the team's image of spirited performance and to help the team determine the characteristics that undergird such spiritedness. Helping the team to translate its images of greatness into concrete actions is the crux of this activity.

Approximate time: 60-90 minutes.

Headline:

_____

_____

Obituary:

_____

_____

_____

_____

_____

_____

_____

_____

_____

_____

_____

_____

_____

_____

_____

_____

_____

_____

_____

_____

_____

_____

_____

_____

Photocopied from _Building Team Spirit_ by Barry Heermann.
Published by McGraw-Hill, ISBN 0-07-028472-5. To order, call 1-800-2MCGRAW.

A VALUES ACTIVITY: RITES OF PASSAGE

Learning Goals

1. To create awareness of the unique phases of life and rites of passage of the team.
2. To identify key values associated with each of the team's life phases.
3. To develop a comprehensive statement of team values.

Preparation

1. Provide three pieces of flip chart paper and four colored markers for every three to five team members.
2. Tear off two-inch strips of masking tape and place the tape on the walls of the room, two strips for each participant in groups of three to five.
3. Create four flip chart displays, with the following headings:

   Key Values: Past Team
   Key Values: Existing Team
   Key Values: Emerging Team
   Key Team Values

Learning Activity

1. Explain that teams have their own unique life phases, and that the purpose of this activity is to create awareness of those phases in the life of the team and the particular rites of passage that this team has passed through or is passing through currently.
2. Organize the team into subteams of three to five. Explain that each subteam will create images, visualizations, or icons for three separate phases in the life of the team—

- the past team,
- the existing team, and
- the emerging team

—using the three sheets of flip chart paper and four color markers provided to them.

3. Clarify that for each phase the subteam should first discuss the most distinct quality, defining characteristic, and climate of the team. After discussing the uniqueness associated with the past team a visual image should be created using the flip chart paper and markers. Then the subteam should discuss the uniqueness associated with the existing team, creating a visual representation, followed by a third visualization for the emerging team. Provide approximately 10 to 15 minutes for work in subteams for each of the three phases, or a total of 30 to 45 minutes. Ask subteams to post their visual images on the walls.

4. Upon completion of the visuals for the three life phases, ask a representative of each subteam to discuss its visuals for each phase, one at a time, beginning with the past. After all the images have been presented, ask what the members perceive to be the outstanding values that operated in the early team and record them on the flip chart you have prepared. Proceed to the presentations of the second and third phases, recording the consensus of the group about the values associated with each phase. Provide approximately 10 to 15 minutes for each phase, or a total of 30 to 45 minutes.

5. After discussing the phases and values, ask the team to draw upon the best of the past, present, and future to write a statement of the team's value system.

6. Ask the team to reflect on the implications of their life phases and key team values. Record the answers on the Key Team Values flip chart.

What to Expect

This activity results in a heightened appreciation among team members for their work together and the values that guide them. Subteams may generate very different interpretations of the three phases. Acknowledge the value of all the interpretations of each subteam, paying particular attention to all the inferences. Successful facilitation of this activity relies on discerning the critical values operating in the past, present, and, most importantly, in the team's anticipated future.

Approximate time: 75-120 minutes.

Learning Goals

1. To assist a mature team in identifying achievements, values, and mistakes that characterize their work together.
2. To support the team in envisioning the future and claiming their role in bringing about that future.

Preparation

Create four flip chart displays with the following headings:

Stories of Team Heights and Depths
Flight of Fancy
Team Assertion
Action Steps

Learning Activity

1. Begin by initiating a brainstorming activity regarding the work of the team over the last decade. Ask team members to tell stories of their past achievements, values, successes, mistakes, and high points, and to reflect on how these contributed to or detracted from the team's sense of meaning and purpose. Record their responses on the flip chart you have prepared. Allow 20 to 30 minutes for this discussion.
2. Request that team members relax, close their eyes, and focus on the work of the team ten years into the future. Ask the team to take a "flight of fancy," imagining that it is ten years into the future and they are flying high above the earth as a bird or in a flying machine of their own design.

119

- What are people doing?
- What are the services and products that the team is providing to its customers?
- How are the customers different?
- How is the team different?
- What other images and impressions do they see?

Record all ideas on the flip chart you have prepared. Allow 20 to 30 minutes for reflection and brainstorming ideas.

3. Ask the team to identify the outstanding patterns of change or progress that emerge from the images. Facilitate their discussion.

4. Based upon the images, ask the team to assert its vision of the future in a single sentence. For example,

- The XYZ team is the world leader in ...
- The ABC team is the foremost provider of ...
- The 123 team is the ultimate developer and deliverer of ...

Allow 20 minutes for this discussion. Record their ideas on the flip chart you have prepared.

5. Request that the team brainstorm action steps for realizing the visions they generated. Record their ideas on the flip chart you have prepared. Allow 20 to 30 minutes for this brainstorming.

What to Expect

Participants generate very different and unique images of their future in this activity, based upon reflection on their past. Help the team to reach agreement about the most compelling images of their intended future. A potential powerful outcome of this activity is the team's vision, expressed in a single sentence.

Approximate time: 90-120 minutes.

5

Claiming Goals and Roles

All ... are caught in an inescapable network of mutuality,
tied in a single garment of destiny ...
I can never be what I ought to be until you are
what you ought to be,and you can never be
what you ought to be until I am what I ought to be.
This is the inter-related structure of reality.
Martin Luther King, Jr.

Claiming realizes the possibilities generated through the Visioning phase of the Team Spirit Spiral. The following descriptors distinguish Visioning and Claiming:

Visioning	**Claiming**
expansive	task oriented
possibilities	predictions
right brain	left brain
wide-angle	zoom
creative	methodical
free-wheeling	focused
visionary	structured
poetic	practical
end point	path
intuitive	analytical
images	goals
holistic	linear
metaphoric	literal

Through Claiming, a team takes ownership of its goals and roles. Claiming establishes the team's path on the journey to extraordinary Service, and it calls for linear, analytical, focused, and task-oriented thinking. Claiming includes the development of competence and the needed resources to fulfill the vision. Spirit is expressed through the commitment, resolve, and solidarity accomplished in the Claiming phase.

There are two key parameters of Claiming: discipline and mindfulness.

Discipline is the act of creating intention and appropriate action. Mindfulness is the act of creating attention. In Western culture we have a distorted view of discipline as something imposed from the outside, from parents, drill sergeants, bosses, our peer group, athletic coaches, clergy, or schoolteachers. This view of other-imposed discipline inhibits the possibilities within spirited teams and within individuals.

Mindfulness is a necessary corollary of discipline. Mindfulness requires focus on this moment, this choice. Mindfulness can feel uncomfortable in a culture invested in distractions. Distractions lead to choices that are superficial and half-hearted, disconnected from the spirit. Choices made with mindfulness, wakefulness, and attentiveness are more fulfilling and successful.

Discipline within spirited teams involves the internal generation of discipline by team members and the team. This internal discipline leads to extraordinary power. It provokes a single-minded focus. It moves mountains. Externally imposed discipline generates intermittent, unpredictable, and often unsatisfactory results, and it keeps the team splintered and members alienated from each other.

The absence of discipline and mindfulness is dispiriting for teams. Too often team members are obsessed with working long hours, desperately attempting to control events, making more and more items urgent, pushing unmercifully for sometimes fleeting results. It is not surprising that the spirit of the team withers and dries up.

Discipline and mindfulness are a powerful combination; together they lead to responsibility, accountability, and grace under pressure. They allow for focus and intensity in the day in, day out choices that define an extraordinary team. Through discipline and mindfulness we connect with the spirit, to inspire and influence our Claiming as individuals and as a team.

Through Claiming, a team defines and creates commitment for its goals and roles, furthering the team's journey to realization of its vision. Claiming is more than the agreement that is established with the organization about what team members and the team can and will do. It is the internally generated assertion that we **can** make a difference, that we will serve brilliantly, being fully awake and attentive. The agreement that the team achieves about the work that is to be done brings a single-minded focus to achieving the organizational support and team member competencies necessary to deliver the chosen goals and roles.

Willingly taking on goals and roles goes beyond grudging compliance or formal acceptance. It is commitment, solidarity, and purposeful intention shared by the team. The learning activities in this chapter are designed to support such powerful Claiming.

The Learning Activities

Sharing Individual and Team Goals allows members of the team to clarify the contexts for their own goals and to consider team goals.

Claiming Mandala: Individual/Team Goals involves team members in creating a visual rendering of prized personal and team goals.

Manifest Destiny fosters multiple perspectives on desired team goals using a modified Delphi approach.

Spirited Role Clarification helps team members appreciate the range of roles across the team, including the aspects of role that possess the greatest spirit.

Spirited Team Accountability helps individual team members to achieve alignment with their roles through the use of a grid that plots key team tasks against team membership.

Core Competencies of Team Members allows team members to assess and share their predisposition toward three core competencies necessary to achieving spirit in the team.

Identifying Team Member Skill Sets and Mind-Sets assists team members in planning their professional development related to a wide range of skills.

Claiming Organization Support provides team members the opportunity to develop strategies for winning organization support.

What to Keep in Mind When Facilitating These Learning Activities

- Support team members in claiming their own internal resources to succeed in their team assignment.
- Support team members in achieving alignment of goals and roles.

- Assist team members in reflecting on and designing strategies for developing themselves for their team positions.

- Assist the team in rallying internal support so as to acquire the necessary resources to accomplish the work of the team.

- Affirm team members' capacity to claim the use of team spirit in the team.

SHARING INDIVIDUAL AND TEAM GOALS

Learning Goals

1. To heighten awareness about ideal conditions for setting individual and team goals and to share experiences and expectations about goal setting.
2. To share individual and team goals.

Preparation

1. Photocopy the Reflections on Individual/Team Goal Development handout for all participants.
2. Create three flip chart displays with the headings:

   Personal Goals
   Factors That Influence Team Goal Setting
   Perceived Team Goals

Learning Activity

1. Clarify to participants that this learning activity will help team members to increase their awareness about influences and preferred contexts for setting individual and team goals.
2. Distribute the Reflections on Individual/Team Goal Development handout. Ask participants to keep the handouts face down until you give the signal to turn them over. Indicate that in a few minutes each team participant will be matched with a colleague to share perspectives regarding goal setting. Participants will share their ideas by providing endings for a series of incomplete sentences that address various aspects of their life and work, including goal setting. Explain that some of the sentences

have to do with team implications or personal implications of goal setting, and some with broader life implications.

3. Instruct the team on the following ground rules:

   a. Partner number one reads sentence number one and completes it with a spontaneous response; partner number two reads sentence number one and completes it; repeat the process for all the sentences.

   b. Team members should keep their full attention on their partners, avoiding the temptation to read ahead.

   c. Partners are to complete the sentences without elaborating on why responses were given in a particular way. (Note: When all sentences have been completed, partners may choose to discuss how and why responses were given.)

   d. Partners are to respond spontaneously to each incomplete sentence with the first thoughts that come to mind.

4. Ask participants if they have any questions. Have them choose partners. When ready, ask the partners to turn their handouts over and begin responding to each incomplete sentence, cycling through to the last sentence. Allow approximately 15 minutes.

5. When all team partners have completed this activity, ask:

   a. What did you notice about yourself or your colleague as a result of completing this activity related to team items? Related to personal items?

   b. What did you notice about how you set and accomplish personal goals? What influences explain your style?

   c. What did you notice about how the team sets and accomplishes its goals? What influences explain the team's style?

   d. What were the personal goals that you identified in this activity?

   e. What were the team goals that you identified in this activity?

   Record participants' personal goals (i.e., item d) on the flip chart you have prepared. (Note: Identify the name of the team member and his or her personal goal.)

6. Discuss the personal goals with the team, providing time for participants to elaborate on their personal destinies.

7. Discuss with the team the factors that influence team goal setting (i.e., item c). Record participants' responses on the flip chart you prepared.

8. Discuss perceived team goals with the group (i.e., item e), providing time for participants to elaborate on why there may have been differences or nonalignment among team members regarding their team goals. Record participants' responses on the flip chart you prepared. Develop consensus among the group regarding what they would like to do to achieve greater goal alignment (if necessary).

9. Ask participants what they have observed about goal setting as a result of this learning activity.

What to Expect

This activity generates considerable energy among participants during the paired sharing. It is important to reinforce the ground rules for the paired sharing to avoid pairs' getting bogged down because of misunderstandings. Successful facilitation of this activity involves moving the team to reach agreement about perceived team goals. If there appears to be a lack of agreement, engage participants in a discussion of team goals or consider the use of one of the Chapter 4 Visioning activities to help clarify team goals.

Approximate time: 60-75 minutes.

Family who know me best say that my biggest accomplishment was ...

Friends who know me best say that my biggest accomplishment was ...

*The most exciting goal that I see for our team is ...

The talent or skill that I rely on to accomplish things in my life is ...

The talent or skill that I would like to develop that would assist me in accomplishing things in my life is ...

*I have the greatest misgiving about our team accomplishing ... [name some team goal]

The person who has done the most to influence my ability to accomplish goals in my life that I care about is ...

The influence that person had on me was ...

*The biggest challenge to our team in accomplishing our goals is ...

The most challenging things that I face in my life now are ...

The most interesting things I am working toward in my life are ...

*The greatest threat to our accomplishing our goals is ...

The single most important goal that I have in my life at this time is ...

The next most important goal that I have in my life at this time is ...

*What we most need to do to achieve our team goals is ...

What I would most like to have (and do not now have) is ...

What I most like to do with my time (away from work) is ...

*What I would most like to see us do to achieve our team goals is ...

*Indicates team-focused items.

Photocopied from *Building Team Spirit* by Barry Heermann.
Published by McGraw-Hill, ISBN 0-07-028472-5. To order, call 1-800-2MCGRAW.

CLAIMING MANDALA: INDIVIDUAL/TEAM GOALS

Learning Goal

To provide an opportunity for all team members to focus on their unique personal goals and team goals for which they experience the greatest passion and to share that passion with team members.

Preparation

1. Photocopy the Claiming Mandala handout for all participants.
2. Tear off sheets of flip chart paper for each participant and place them in an out-of-the-way place.
3. Tear off two-inch strips of masking tape and place the tape on the walls of the room, two strips for each participant, in groups of four to six.
4. Provide magic markers, enough for each participant to have access to four or more colors.

Learning Activity

1. Begin by explaining that a mandala is a visual representation of prized values, beliefs, and viewpoints held by individuals and groups that captures their essence or "spirit," and that it is an art form commonly found in India (this will be important to identify if the Personal Mandala or the Team Mandala learning activities in Chapters 3 and 4 were not used).
2. Distribute the Claiming Mandala handout. Discuss the display of the Claiming Mandala that appears on the handout. Provide participants with sheets of flip chart paper and a variety of colored markers, and then ask them to think of and then draw an image (icon or archetype) that captures a strongly held personal goal, as shown on the handout. Ask participants to do the same for a team goal that they particularly prize or

that they believe holds important promise for the team. Ask participants to put their names on the tops of the flip chart pages. Allow approximately 15 minutes for participants to complete their Claiming Mandalas, composed of the two goal images.

3. After the mandalas have been completed, assign participants to teams of four to six. Designate a separate area of the room for each team. Identify the location of the masking tape positioned around the room so that the mandalas can be taped to the wall.

4. Within the small groups, participants describe both their personal and team goals, explaining why they chose these goals. Allow 10 to 15 minutes for this sharing.

5. Reassemble the full group. Ask each participant to briefly share his or her Claiming Mandala:

   a.   Allow participants to describe why their personal goals are important in their lives.

   b.   Allow participants to describe why their team goals are important to the success of the team. Allow approximately one to two minutes per person or 15 to 25 minutes for the full team for this sharing.

6. Ask participants what they have observed about personal and team goals as a result of this learning activity.

What to Expect

Using graphic images to display personal and team goals taps into a different level of knowing that is valued in the lives of the participants. If there is a concern that participants may not have developed sufficient personal awareness to reveal important personal goals, it may be useful to select an activity from Chapter 4 on personal Visioning to help develop this awareness. A key component of this activity is the sharing.

Approximate time: 60-75 minutes.

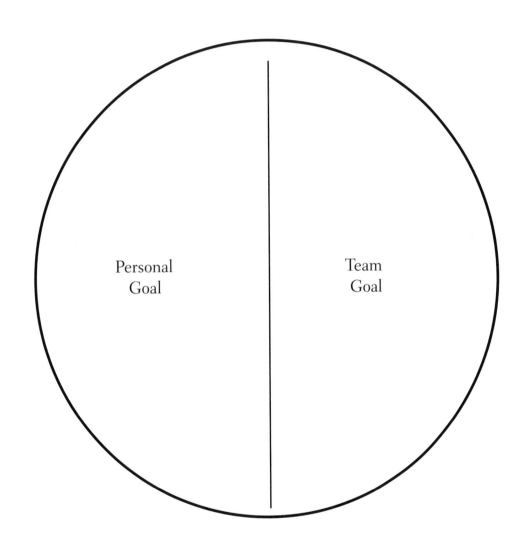

Personal
Goal

Team
Goal

MANIFEST DESTINY

Learning Goal

To list team goals and rank them in order of importance.

Preparation

1. Provide six 3x5 cards for each team member.
2. Create two flip chart displays with the headings, Most Compelling Goals and Action Steps.

Learning Activity

1. Ask team members to record on 3x5 cards up to six ultimate destinies (goals)—one goal to a card—that they would like to see the team embrace, and sign their names. Allow approximately 10 to 15 minutes for generating ideas.
2. When all team members have recorded their ideas regarding ultimate team destinies, collect the cards and randomly shuffle them, then distribute six completed cards to each person. Request that team members add ideas, pose questions, and make constructive comments on all of the cards that they received, and then pass them along. Allow approximately 20 to 40 minutes for circulating and making comments on cards.
3. Return the cards to the owners after the cards have circulated through the entire team. Participants then review comments made by their team colleagues.
4. Based on the exchange of ideas recorded on the cards, lead the team in a discussion of the goals they generated. Ask the team to brainstorm a list of the most compelling goals that will empower the team to achieve

its vision. Ask the team to rank the goals by importance. Record the goals and their rankings on the flip chart you have prepared.

5. Ask the team to identify action steps necessary to accomplish one or two of their key goals. Record their responses on the flip chart you have prepared.

What to Expect

This is an excellent activity for generating goals that support the team's mission or purpose. The key facilitation task is to achieve consensus about the most compelling goals that will help the team to powerfully accomplish its vision and purpose. This activity is particularly useful for start-up teams.

Approximate time: 60-90 minutes.

Learning Goals

1. To clarify the critical roles of each team member as perceived by the team.
2. To allow all team members to reflect and comment on the critical roles of their colleagues.

Preparation

1. Provide a sheet of flip chart paper and four colored magic markers for each participant (red, blue, black, and green).
2. Tear off two-inch strips of masking tape and place the tape on the walls of the room, two strips for each participant.

Learning Activity

1. Request that all team members create a flip chart display with their names at the top and a list of their individual roles and responsibilities, underlining with a green magic marker those roles that provide them with the greatest passion and spirit, and in red the roles that they would happily be rid of. Further, ask participants to underline in blue those roles in which the participant would appreciate assistance and learning to help fulfill the task. Allow approximately 10 to 15 minutes for creating these displays.
2. After all team members have finished their flip chart displays, have them hang the displays up around the training room.
3. Ask team members to circulate, silently reading the roles and responsibilities on each chart. Ask them to make notes directly on the displays,

adding constructive comments, raising questions, adding ideas and suggestions. Allow approximately 20 to 40 minutes for team members to circulate and make comments.

4. Following this round of activity, have the team members discuss their respective roles, attempting to see how they might provide mutual support and achieve greater synergy and spirit. Allow approximately 20 to 40 minutes for this discussion.

5. Ask team members to reflect on their experience in examining team roles.

What to Expect

This activity provides a wonderful opportunity for team members to share their work with colleagues, indicating the passion as well as the drudgery present for them in their work. Full disclosure of these various elements of each member's role allows other team members to provide support and to effectively align their work to accomplish the team's objective.

Approximate time: 60-90 minutes.

SPIRITED TEAM ACCOUNTABILITY

Learning Goals

1. To identify and clarify critical communication and authority aspects of each member's role.
2. To allow all team members to reflect and comment on the roles of their colleagues.

Preparation

1. Prior to facilitating this exercise request that the team leader or your team liaison provide you with a list of the key tasks of the team from his or her perspective.
2. Create a flip chart display composed of a grid, with columns and rows, with the names of all team members along one axis and the critical tasks of the team along the other axis.
3. Create a flip chart display defining the symbols in item three below, and post it in a prominent place in the room.
4. Provide a set of red, green, blue, black, and purple markers for each team member.
5. Provide notepaper for participants.

Learning Activity

1. Present the flip chart displays of the grid and the symbols to the team, and review the purpose of the activity. Engage the team in a discussion of the key tasks of the team. Modify the list of tasks if differences emerge from this discussion. Allow approximately 15 minutes for this discussion.

139

2. Ask the team members to consider their roles in relationship to each task, assigning symbols for each task on the notepaper provided.

3. Request that each team member record the symbol that best describes his or her relationship with each of the team tasks on the flip chart display:

   a purple star for tasks for which the team member is accountable;

   a black question mark for tasks the team member would like to be kept informed about;

   a green exclamation point for tasks the team member is responsible for carrying out;

   a blue plus sign for tasks the team member is willing to provide support to others for;

   a red spiral for tasks the team member feels the greatest spirit for.

4. Ask the team to evaluate the pattern of responses for each cell in the Team Accountabilities grid. Facilitate the discussion among team members, reconciling differences in understanding, encouraging new patterns of work among team members, and contributing to greater alignment of roles among team members.

What to Expect

This activity is an excellent way for teams to create understanding and alignment of their roles, and heighten awareness of the ways that team members communicate with and support each other. The key in facilitating this activity is in guiding the discussion after the matrix has been completed by all team members. Work through each critical task, one by one, suggesting that questions or concerns that only affect a few team members be handled at another time. Focus on achieving alignment and agreement among team members regarding all of the tasks identified. This is an extremely useful activity for new teams, and for mature teams that have modified their charter.

Approximate time: 60-90 Minutes.

CORE COMPETENCIES OF TEAM MEMBERS

Learning Goals

1. To foster awareness of core competencies associated with the three modes of thinking that are the basis of team spirit: organization, science, and spirit.
2. To discern the strengths of team members related to the three competencies.

Preparation

1. Prepare a lecturette regarding the three modes of thinking from which team spirit was developed: organization, science, and spirit (see lecturette at the end of this activity).
2. Photocopy the Competencies handout for all participants.
3. Prepare a flip chart display with the two questions identified in item five below.
4. Tear off sheets of flip chart paper for each participant and place them in an out-of-the-way place.
5. Tear off two-inch strips of masking tape and place the tape on the walls of the room, two strips for each participant, in groups of four to six.
6. Provide a set of four colored magic markers for each participant.

Learning Activity

1. Present a lecturette regarding the three modes of thinking from which team spirit was developed: organization, science, and spirit. Engage team participants in a discussion of these three modes of thinking. Allow 10 to 15 minutes for the lecturette and discussion.

2. Explain that in this activity participants will reflect on their predispositions toward each of the three modes of thinking in a team environment, analyzing their strengths related to each mode.

3. Suggest that within each of these three modes of thinking there is critical team member competency that will be the focus of this activity. Distribute the Competencies handout. Facilitate a discussion regarding the distinguishing features and the requisite skills associated with each of these competencies:

    Organization: *ways of doing* the organizational work that is required, e.g., technical and interpersonal skills;

    Science: *ways of knowing* (methodology) that promote rigorous analytical thinking, e.g., linear, structured, rational processes;

    Spirit: *ways of being* (holistic, intuitive, synergistic, metaphoric awareness), e.g., inner wisdom and purpose to serve.

    Allow 10 minutes for this discussion.

4. Clarify that these three broad areas of competence are all necessary for spirited teams. One competency is not preferable to the other. We all have strengths in all three areas, but we tend to have a preference for one or a combination of these competencies.

5. Ask participants to reflect on each of the three areas of competence, recording their thoughts on the handout provided. Instruct participants to consider the following as they probe their experience in each of the three areas:

    a. Which competency area do you tend to be drawn to immediately and why?

    b. What skills and awareness do you possess for each area of competency?

    Allow 10 to 15 minutes for reflection and writing.

6. When all participants have finished writing, ask them to turn to their neighbor and share what they have discovered about these competencies in themselves. Allow eight minutes for this sharing, four minutes for each person, indicating when 30 seconds remain in each four-minute round.

7. Ask the participants to prepare a presentation of their respective competencies using the flip chart paper and magic markers provided. Request that each team member draw an image (icon or archetype) that captures the essence of the competency, or combination of competencies, that he or she most strongly relies upon in their work in the team,

placing the image in the middle of the page. Surrounding the image, ask participants to record in words their analysis of their outstanding strengths in each of the three areas of competency. Ask participants to put their names on the tops of their flip chart pages. Allow approximately 15 minutes for participants to complete this work.

8. When all participants have completed the assignment, ask that they form smaller teams of four to six persons. Designate a separate area of the room for each team, where masking tape has been positioned so that flip chart displays can be taped to the wall.

9. Within the small groups, have participants describe their visual images as well as their analyses of skills and awareness for all three competencies. Allow 10 to 15 minutes for this sharing.

10. Reassemble the full group. Ask each participant to briefly share his or her image of primary competency, and briefly refer to skills and awareness in all three areas of competency.

What to Expect

Participants are often less clear about the science and spirit competencies and have a better understanding of organizational competency. Focus on each competency and give examples. Reinforce the idea that all team members draw from all three areas, but that one or more of these areas tend to be more critical to an individual than the others. This is an excellent activity for emphasizing the uniqueness of each team member.

Approximate time: 90-120 minutes.

1. Organization—*ways of doing* the organizational work that is required (e.g., technical and interpersonal skills)

_____

_____

_____

_____

_____

2. Science—*ways of knowing* (methodology) that promote rigorous analytical thinking (e.g., linear, structured, rational processes)

_____

_____

_____

_____

_____

3. Spirit—*ways of being* (holistic, intuitive, synergistic, metaphoric awarenesses) (e.g., inner wisdom and purpose to serve).

_____

_____

_____

_____

_____

Photocopied from *Building Team Spirit* by Barry Heermann.
Published by McGraw-Hill, ISBN 0-07-028472-5. To order, call 1-800-2MCGRAW.

LECTURETTE

The Interplay of Organization, Science, and Spirit

Key point number one: Team spirit draws from thinking about organization, science, and spirit.

There is a growing appreciation for how the seemingly opposite considerations of organization, science, and spirit are interdependent and mutually inclusive. *Building Team Spirit* integrates thinking about spirit with current thinking about team and organization development, as well as thinking about science. The synthesis is suggested in the following:

Organization: Contemporary thinking from the field of organizational development about how teams move through developmental phases and can be cultivated to work more effectively.

Science: Disciplined scientific investigation of life, from the smallest organism to the universe itself, has revealed similar and identifiable evolutionary patterns.

Spirit: The urge to find meaning and purpose and the interconnections between human beings are important to people around the world and across time.

These three areas may seem divergent, yet they share a common core. Each creates wholeness out of separateness; each offers a unique contribution to the process of bonding that must occur before a team can function at a high performance level.

Key point number two: Thinking regarding organization.

In 1988, team development consultants Allan Drexler and David Sibbett conceptualized a team development model called the "team performance model." Drexler and Sibbett suggested that all teams pass through stages of development. Each stage presents the team with particular concerns. For each stage, Drexler and Sibbett describe the behaviors that signal whether the concerns peculiar to that stage have been resolved. If such concerns are not resolved, the team is "stuck" at that stage, requiring resolution before it can move on to later stages.

Drexler and Sibbett facilitated team development based upon this model. Teams and organizations benefited from having a shared model and vocabulary through which they could understand the phases and stages of their development as a team.

From Sibbett and Drexler, *Building Team Spirit* draws the idea that a team is something evolved over time, with necessary phases that lead to team effectiveness. *Building Team Spirit* also acknowledges the importance of a shared model and vocabulary that teams can draw upon to understand and enhance their work together.

Key point number three: Thinking regarding science.

In 1992, Margaret Wheatley, drawing upon the work of general systems theorist Eric Jantsch, wrote about organization disequilibrium (referred to as dissonance in *Building Team Spirit*), affirming it as inherently life-giving and nurturing.

The acceptance and resolution of dissonance, Wheatley argues, is the process that permits systems to regenerate and move to higher levels of awareness and effectiveness. Eric Jantsch calls this process "self-organization."

Each team is similar to a living organism. At every moment in time it has its own blend of forces, some consonant and some dissonant. Teams do not evolve by suppressing their dissonance; rather, they move to higher levels of effectiveness by understanding and embracing it.

From Margaret Wheatley, *Building Team Spirit* takes the idea that the disequilibrium within a team or organization provides an energy source capable of moving the organization to a higher level of awareness and effectiveness. It is this disequilibrium that we must learn to embrace.

Key point number four: Thinking regarding spirit.

Matthew Fox, a key investigator of spirit in work, integrates ideas from ancient traditions with more recent thinking about spirit (1994). Fox points to native and traditional peoples' capacity to recognize and celebrate "awe and wonder" as a group experience. Further, he emphasizes the cleansing force that comes from recognizing the darker, more difficult manifestations of the group experience.

We can be brought to vivid awareness of these two values through a process Fox calls "creation storytelling." Such storytelling grounds us in a history of how we arrived at our present, awakens within us awe and wonder at the fact of our being here, and permits the "letting go" that allows expression of the dissonant elements of the group experience.

Through Matthew Fox, *Building Team Spirit* lays claim to the importance of transcendence, through the team's capacity to share "awe and wonder" and the capacity for cleansing that lies within the group. The Spiral explicitly identifies the phases of Celebrating and Letting Go.

Learning Goals

1. To identify team members' skill sets for performing their work.
2. To clarify team members' mind sets (deeper intuitive awareness) for performing their work.

Preparation

1. Create a flip chart display with a vertical line down the middle of the page and two headings at the top of each column, Skill Sets and Mind-Sets.
2. Create a flip chart display with the heading, Action Steps.

Note: Because this activity assumes understanding of the Team Spirit Spiral, use one of the following activities from Appendix D as a prelude to this activity: Walk in Nature: Discovering the Phases of the Spiral or The Seasons of a Team's Life: Establishing Team Climate.

Learning Activity

1. Distinguish between skill sets (technical and interpersonal skills) and mind-sets (deeper intuitive awarenesses and skills of the spirit). Note that in many work settings the preoccupation is with technical skills, and that in the last decade there has been increased awareness of the importance of interpersonal skills. Suggest that mind-sets—intuitive awareness and skills of the spirit—are needed to achieve the deep levels of communication and collaboration necessary to achieve high performance.
2. Explain that in this activity participants will explore both skills sets and mind-sets to determine what the team needs and wants from team members to ensure spirited, high performance.

149

3. Ask the team to begin brainstorming those skills in both areas that are required of this team to be a truly spirited team. Refer to the phases of the Team Spirit Spiral to stimulate thinking. Record their responses on the flip chart display. Allow 15 to 20 minutes for this brainstorming.

4. Ask the team to prioritize the skills in each column in order of importance.

5. Next, request that the team brainstorm action steps that it needs to take to develop the requisite skills identified in both areas. Record their responses on the flip chart display. Allow 15 minutes for this brainstorming.

6. Ask if there are any insights or awareness that team members would like to share as a result of completing this learning activity.

What to Expect

It is easier for team members to perceive skill sets that are important to the team than mind-sets. Probe with the team the kind of awareness that it must possess in the realm of mind-sets to perform its work brilliantly. This activity is most successful to the extent that mind-sets that are important to team success are identified and celebrated. Fully acknowledge the team's possession of both skill sets and mind-sets.

Approximate time: 60 minutes.

CLAIMING ORGANIZATION SUPPORT

Learning Goals

1. To determine the resources needed to become a spirited, high-performing team.
2. To develop strategies for obtaining the organization support for these needs.

Preparation

Create four flip chart displays, with the following headings:

Resource Needs
Network of Support
Strategy for Achieving Organization Support
Action Steps

Learning Activity

1. Ask the team to brainstorm the resources it needs to be an extraordinary team. Suggest that they not limit their thinking in any way. Record their ideas on the first flip chart display. Allow 15 to 20 minutes for this brainstorming.
2. Suggest that what is important as a backdrop for thinking about how to achieve their needs is consideration of the network of support that they currently have or would like to have in the organization. Request that they look to all parts of the organization, to peer relationships with persons in other teams, to suppliers, to customers, to leaders and others with positions of influence, to opinion leaders in the organization, etc.

Record their thinking on the second flip chart display. Allow 15 to 20 minutes for this brainstorming.

3. Based upon this investigation into the network of support, request that the team brainstorm strategies to engage and enroll persons identified in their network of support. Record their strategy ideas on the third flip chart display. Allow 15 to 20 minutes for this inquiry and brainstorming.

4. Ask the team to consider the action steps it now needs to take. Record these action steps on the last flip chart display. Allow 15 to 20 minutes for this brainstorming.

5. Ask if there are any insights or awareness that team members would like to share as a result of completing this activity.

What to Expect

This activity helps teams to identify what resources they need and the gatekeepers who are the keys to getting those resources. Successful facilitation of this activity lies in developing effective communication strategies for gaining the attention of and motivating those gatekeepers to respond to the need for resources.

Approximate time: 90-120 minutes.

6

Celebrating Team Accomplishment

Let the beauty we love be what we do.
There are a hundred ways
to kneel and kiss the ground.
Rumi

Members of spirited, high-performing teams celebrate their accomplishments, individually and collectively. Celebrating is a critical force that animates and sustains team performance. Learning to appreciate the team and team members, their uniqueness and differences, is essential to fostering team spirit. Teams that omit attention to Celebrating are unconscious and unappreciative of the potential of the people, resources, and opportunities in their midst and greatly inhibit their capacity to become extraordinary.

To celebrate effectively requires a generous spirit in both giving and receiving. The art of receiving recognition is distinct from that of giving recognition. Giving recognition requires being aware of what is working in the team and expressing appreciation. Getting recognition requires active listening, fully receiving the positive messages expressed by others. Recognition transforms team relationships.

Far too many teams and organizations focus on what is not working, on problems, on who is wrong and what needs fixing. In Celebrating, we create positive team relationships and change the environment in which the team performs its work to one that is results-oriented and supportive of its members. Celebrating promotes individual and team spirit, heightened optimism, energy, joy, and passion for work. It allows for purposeful, committed action.

There is power in affirmation and recognition, creating a climate of appreciation that fosters growth, healing, and achievement. The Hawthorne experiments (experiments at the Hawthorne Electric Plant that serendipitously revealed that attention to workers resulted in increased performance by those workers) confirmed that paying attention to employees results in higher performance. Medical studies using placebos confirm that if patients believe the "pills" will make them better, they get better. Children randomly identified as high-achieving students are reported by teachers to perform at higher levels than students not identified as high-achieving.

Celebrating within teams means actively communicating recognition and positive regard for the work of the team. It is not about fixing. It is about constant acknowledgment of the best we can be, and about what is great about team members and the team.

"Wonder" is a dimension of Celebrating that operates powerfully in high-performing teams. When wonder is present team members report a kind of ecstasy, a feeling of being swept away, fully experiencing the team's greatness, and being connected with a sense of joy, passion, life, and wholeness. Wonder acknowledges the power of the team to transform the present and to create a powerful future.

Wonder is a quality of spirit that operates within high-performing teams. It requires nurturing and development. The activities in this chapter are designed to foster Celebrating.

The Learning Activities

Fostering Celebration: An Interview and Discussion Process involves team members in an extended activity that encourages deep reflection on the greatness inherent in the team.

Team Creation Stories allows team members to tell their stories of team formation and the initial rite of passage of the team, clarifying the importance of Celebrating.

Honoring Team Accomplishments: A Retrospective assists team members in identifying and graphically portraying the successes the team has realized since its inception.

Celebrating: Past and Present Stories of Team Success encourages team members to tell their stories of team success throughout the history of their work together, transferring that awareness into the present.

Celebration Letter engages team members in identifying a key person who influenced the team and preparing a letter that acknowledges the person's contribution to the team.

Honoring Team Members involves team members in an acknowledgment of the contributions of each team member to the work of the team.

Celebration Teams allows the team to plan a celebration honoring the team's spirit and achievement.

Spirit Award results in a tangible acknowledgment of a person or persons on the team who have contributed significantly to the spirit of the team.

What to Keep in Mind When Facilitating These Learning Activities

- Model Celebrating in your work with the team, liberally acknowledging participants for their contributions.
- Assist the team in developing concrete ways to celebrate their accomplishments
- Celebrate the uniqueness and differences of team members

Learning Goals

1. To help the team realize the importance of Celebrating, nurturing celebration based on the team's record of achievement.
2. To design action steps for ongoing Celebrating within the team.

Preparation

1. Arrange for meeting space for separate interviews with each team member, in addition to the usual meeting room.
2. Arrange to have notepaper or a laptop computer for recording the
responses from team member interviews.
3. Create four flip chart displays with the following headings:

What Individuals Contributed to Team Spirit
What the Team Contributed to Team Spirit
What the Organization Contributed to Team Spirit
Action Steps

4. Note: See Visioning, Chapter 4, Celebrating Where We Are and Going
Beyond, as a potential follow-up to this learning activity.

Learning Activity

Note: This learning activity occurs in two phases. The first phase involves
interviews with each team member and the second phase involves facilitation with the full team.

Phase I: Individual Interviews

1. Conduct separate 30-minute interviews with each team member. During each interview session explain that the purpose of the interview is to identify where the team member feels the greatest spirit in his or her work on the team and where the team as a whole finds its greatest spirit. The session is not designed to examine problems or areas of concern.

2. Request that all team members interviewed reflect on what is working for them regarding their participation on this team. What do they like about being on the team? When do they feel most full of spirit, enlivened, empowered, excited, on fire, and assured? Under what circumstances do they experience the greatest spirit and personal satisfaction? Actively work to prompt and encourage the team members to recreate their experiences of being spirit-filled.

3. Ask each team member to reflect on what is working for the team as a whole in their work together. What do team members as a whole appreciate about being on the team? When is the team as a whole most full of spirit, enlivened, empowered, excited, on fire, and assured? Under what circumstances does the team as a whole experience the greatest spirit and personal satisfaction? Actively work to prompt and encourage the team member to recreate the team's experience of spirit.

4. Keep careful notes on the concrete incidents and circumstances that are identified. Freely share your enthusiasm for the incidents that team members report about themselves and about the team, i.e., do not assume a value-neutral position.

5. When all interviews are completed, prepare a report that notes patterns and common threads of spirited performance. This report will serve as the basis for a feedback session that you will provide during the full group meeting.

Phase II: Full Group

1. Explain that the purpose of this learning activity is to identify where team members experience the greatest spirit in their work together—as individuals and as a team—and to begin the practice of Celebrating these times of spirit in order to encourage higher levels of spiritedness and celebration.

2. Present your feedback report, noting the key incidents of team spirit reported in the interviews. Present to the team moments of spiritedness

and appreciation. Report exact circumstances when the team felt most full of spirit, enlivened, empowered, excited, and on fire. Avoid a monologue. Work to prompt and encourage team members to recreate the team's experience of being spirited throughout your report.

3. As a means of encouraging full participation of all team members, periodically request that team members consider specifically what they contributed, what the team contributed, and what the larger organization contributed to facilitate such spirit. Record these insights on the first three flip chart displays placed in the front of the room. Be sensitive to the spirit of the team as it discusses its moments of greatness, facilitating a crescendo of appreciation in the discussion. Allow at least 60 minutes for this session. Take more time as needed.

4. When the team has exhausted examination of its spiritedness, ask the team to consider what it learned about the power of celebration. Ask the team to observe the relationship of Celebrating to spirited, high-performing teams.

5. Conclude by asking the team to identify concrete action steps that it might take to maintain an environment of celebration. Record these insights on the last flip chart display.

What to Expect

Offering an opportunity to meet with team members to discuss realities of the team can lead to complaints, upsets, disappointments, etc. Be careful to see that this does not happen. Clarify that venting frustrations is not the focus of this activity. In this activity, good facilitation requires something other than the normal value-neutral posture that is typical in organization development diagnosis. What is appropriate is full expression of your enthusiasm for the spirited moments that participants identify in their sharing. Probe the importance of moments of spirited work in the team, supporting the experience of celebration.

During the facilitation of the full team component of this activity, assist in building a crescendo of team spirit by Celebrating the reports from individual interviews and through full group discussion. Feedback from the facilitator that the team is doing great work is extremely important, helping to change the prevailing conversation in many teams from what is not working to what is working, and Celebrating the team's good works.

Approximate time: 60-120 minutes (exclusive of interview phase).

TEAM CREATION STORIES

Learning Goal

To provide an opportunity to celebrate the team's creation story focusing on the "awe and wonder" present during the initial formation stages.

Preparation

Create three flip chart displays with the headings, Creation Stories, Critical Team Qualities, and Ways to Embrace Team Qualities.

Learning Activity

1. As background, explain that the creation story is a time-honored technique for strengthening unity and affirming membership within a family, tribe, or other cohesive group. It can be used effectively to enhance the sense of membership in teams.

2. Ask team members to return to their earliest memories of team formation and development, recounting particular stories of deliberations and discussions that were pivotal in shaping the group, its process, and its relationship with the surrounding organization.

3. Request that the team reflect on moments of awe and wonder, fun and intrigue during this early period of the team's development. Encourage a spirit of celebration as members recall their stories. Record specific events and recollections on the flip chart display you have prepared as they are remembered by the team. Allow approximately 15 minutes for this discussion.

4. Based upon this reflection on the team's creation story, ask the team to name those critical qualities of teamwork that were developed during the team's formation phase, recording their ideas on the second flip chart display. Allow approximately 15 minutes for this discussion.

5. Request that the team identify those critical qualities of teamwork that are currently not present. Ask the team to identify ways that it might embrace some of those qualities that are not now present in their work. Record their ideas on the third flip chart display. Allow approximately 15 minutes for this discussion.

What to Expect

This activity generates excitement around the team's beginnings. The key to successful facilitation of this activity is getting the team to connect to prized memories and their underlying values that are associated with the birth of the team and with their current work. Focus especially on the team's incorporating some of those qualities that are now absent in their work together.

Approximate time: 60-90 minutes.

ACTIVITY
HONORING TEAM ACCOMPLISHMENTS: A RETROSPECTIVE

Learning Goal

To identify the major accomplishments of the team and to acknowledge individual members who contributed to the accomplishments.

Preparation

1. Create a flip chart display with the heading, Team Accomplishments.
2. Provide a sheet of flip chart paper for each participant.
3. Provide a set of four colored magic markers for each participant.

Learning Activity

1. Ask team members to identify the major accomplishments of the team since its inception, recording each accomplishment on a flip chart. Work with the team to identify as many accomplishments as there are members of the team; that is, if there are nine team members, have the team identify nine compelling accomplishments. Record the accomplishments on the flip chart display. Allow approximately 20 minutes for this discussion.
2. Let each team member select one of the accomplishments from the list. Instruct them to visualize an image or impression that symbolizes that accomplishment. Have them draw those images or impressions on flip chart paper. Request that they only use images, avoiding words. Allow approximately 15 minutes for the drawing of images.
3. When everyone is finished ask team members to describe their images. Allow approximately 20 minutes for these presentations.
4. Ask team members to identify the most prized elements of teamwork that are exemplified in their images. Ask the team to acknowledge current members of the team who contributed to the accomplishments. Allow approximately 20 minutes for discussion and acknowledgments.

What to Expect

This activity is designed to celebrate the major accomplishments of the team through images, tapping into a deeper level of knowing. Expect some resistance from "non-artists." Keep the momentum up. The creation and presentation of images of accomplishments stimulates high levels of enthusiasm for the work of the team.

Approximate time: 60-90 minutes.

Learning Goals

1. To tell stories of team effectiveness.
2. To design actions that translate the sense of possibility that these stories engender into the day-to-day routine of the team.

Preparation

1. Provide notepaper for all participants.
2. Create two flip chart displays with the headings, Threads and Action Ideas.

Learning Activity

1. Ask individual team members to describe, on the notepaper provided, a time in the life of the team when the team felt potent, alive, full of spirit, fresh, vital, and full of possibility. Request that they tell the story of this time, using the journalistic Who, What, Where, When, Why, and How framework. Allow 15 minutes for reflection and writing.

2. When all team members have finished, ask that they tell their stories. Take the time to hear from all team members. As the stories are told, listen for patterns. Work to achieve consensus about the underlying thread or threads that run through the stories. Record these threads or themes on the first flip chart display.

3. Ask the team to consider what in the life of the team right now could or does generate this quality of spirit. Facilitate an inquiry among team members. Ask what action steps the team could create to reinforce and

extend this sense of spirit, possibility, and greatness. Record their action ideas on the second flip chart display.

4. Request that participants reflect on their experience of storytelling and their action ideas, identifying implications for their work together.

What to Expect

This activity generates considerable energy and a celebratory team mood. The key to successful facilitation of this activity is helping the team to move from the stories of spirited team performance in the past to discovering the source of that spirit in their current work together. The benefit of this experience is established through action steps to continue support for spirited team performance.

Approximate time: 60-90 minutes.

CELEBRATION LETTER

Learning Goals

1. To foster understanding of the importance of acknowledgment for enhanced team performance.
2. To provide an opportunity for team members to practice Celebrating through acknowledgment of a coworker or customer.

Preparation

1. Create a flip chart display with the heading, Good Recognition.
2. Provide writing paper, envelopes, and stamps for all participants.

Learning Activity

1. Lead an open discussion on the importance of acknowledging colleagues, customers, and team leaders. Ask participants for ways they have been acknowledged for their efforts. What makes a good acknowledgment? Record their ideas on the flip chart display. Allow approximately 20 minutes for this discussion.
2. Based upon this discussion, ask team members to write a letter to a coworker or customer who has significantly enhanced the performance of the team.
3. Suggest that writers focus on a specific result that was produced and how that result benefited others. Emphasize that the letters should describe the regard that the writer holds for the specific contribution of the coworker or customer. Allow approximately 15 minutes for letter writing.
4. Have a few team members read their letters.

5. Ask the participants: Did this activity cause you to think of other individuals you would like to acknowledge? How might acknowledgment of this sort be incorporated into your work situation?

6. Encourage team members to mail the letters.

What to Expect

Participants enjoy composing and sharing letters of recognition to people who have important business relationships to the team or organization. Effective facilitation includes assisting the team in translating their positive experience in recognizing a colleague to their ongoing work relationships. Probe with team members the correlation of recognition to spirited, high-performing teams.

Approximate time: 60 minutes.

HONORING TEAM MEMBERS

Learning Goals

1. To celebrate the team's accomplishment of a project.
2. To acknowledge specific contributions of individual team members.

Preparation

1. With the team leader or your team liaison, identify a recent project that was a major accomplishment for the team.
2. Create a flip chart display with two columns, labeling them, Key Actions and Key Lessons.

Learning Activity

1. For a recently completed, successful project, ask the team to list the most important actions that led to success, probing each for the important lessons that resulted. Work with the group to acknowledge what they accomplished and what they learned. Record both key actions and key lessons learned from the project on the flip chart display. Allow approximately 20 minutes for this discussion.
2. Ask the team to sit in a circle. One member of the team is identified as the focus person and the remaining team members provide brief acknowledgments of the contributions that person has made to the group. Emphasizing the importance of generous receiving of acknowledgment and praise from others, instruct the team member serving as the focus person not to respond verbally to the acknowledgment, but rather to simply listen and hear what is being said. One by one, each member of the group becomes the focus person and receives acknowl-

edgment from the team. Allow approximately 20 minutes for the acknowledgment of team members.

3. Have the team return to their seats around the table and ask how they felt about the activity. Ask team members to identify what they learned about themselves, the team, and the project as a result of the activity.

What to Expect

This activity is effectively used at the culmination of a key project. It generates high levels of celebration within the team. Critical learning occurs after all acknowledgments have been communicated and the team inquires into the implications of acknowledging colleagues for achieving high-performance results.

Approximate time: 60 minutes.

ACTIVITY

CELEBRATION TEAMS

Learning Goal

To heighten team spirit through a conscious reflection on the team's work by planning and holding a celebration to commemorate the team.

Preparation

Photocopy the Celebration Parameters handout for all participants.

Learning Activity

Note: This learning activity takes place in two phases, a planning phase and an implementation phase, separated in time by several hours or an intervening day.

Planning Phase

1. Ask the team to divide itself into two equal subteams to plan a celebration to commemorate its work together.
2. The celebration should acknowledge and ritualize "the spirit of the team" in ways that the subteam sees it operating within their work together, acknowledging milestones achieved and significant results accomplished.
3. Distribute the Celebration Parameters handout. Review the parameters for the celebrations and determine if there are any questions.

   Note: Adjust the parameters to meet the limitations of the particular training environment—add or delete items as appropriate.
4. Request that the subteams meet to plan their celebrations. Explain that they will be provided additional time to meet at the beginning of their next session. Emphasize that any material needs should be taken care of

between the end of this session and the beginning of the next session. Allow approximately 20 to 30 minutes for celebration planning.

5. When the planning is complete, bring the planning phase to an end by asking if there are any questions. Determine which team will kick off the celebrations during the next session or the next day.

Implementation Phase

1. Begin by allowing the subteams time to finalize their celebration plans. Allow approximately 10 to 20 minutes for celebration planning.

2. When both subteams are ready, let the celebrations begin. Allow approximately 35 to 50 minutes for celebrations.

3. After both teams have completed their celebrations, have the whole team convene for reflection on the experience. Discuss the importance of celebration for the renewal of team spirit. What did team members find to be particularly meaningful? What did they learn from the process of preparing the celebration?

What to Expect

This powerful activity emphasizes the importance of Celebrating. When initially setting up the activity some participants may question what the celebrations are designed to celebrate. Merely repeat the instructions (i.e., "The celebration should acknowledge and ritualize 'the spirit of the team' in ways that the team sees it operating within their work together."). Emphasize that participants can celebrate anything that is related to the achievements of the team. Reinforce the ground rules.

Approximate time: 30 minutes (planning phase); 60 minutes (implementation phase).

Celebration Parameters

• The celebration should take no longer than 20 minutes.

• It must take place in the training room.

• Each subteam will have 5 minutes to set up the room.

• Cost of materials for the celebration should not exceed $20.

• All special audio-visual requirements need to be handled by the sub-team.

• No lighted candles, food, or beverages are permitted.

• Each subteam needs to plan for a quick 5-minute clean-up after its presentation.

Photocopied from *Building Team Spirit* by Barry Heermann.
Published by McGraw-Hill, ISBN 0-07-028472-5. To order, call 1-800-2MCGRAW.

Learning Goals

1. To understand the importance of acknowledgment to the overall development of a spirited team.
2. To acknowledge the contributions of individuals who contributed significantly to the spirit of the team.

Preparation

Create a flip chart display with the heading, Symbols of Spirit.

Learning Activity

Note: This activity takes place in two phases, a planning phase and an implementation phase.

Planning Phase

1. Discuss with the team the importance of acknowledging individuals who contribute to the team through their spirit. Stress that high performing teams routinely recognize individual members' contributions.
2. Ask team members to brainstorm what might be an appropriate symbol to demonstrate appreciation to an individual team member, recording their ideas on the flip chart display. Reach consensus on a suitable symbol and then discuss ways to manifest this symbol in a concrete way as an award. Allow approximately 15 to 20 minutes for discussion.
3. Request that the team determine how the award might be presented. (For example, it might be passed through the team, member to member; it might be awarded each month; or the award might be presented during staff or quarterly meetings.) Work with the team to achieve consen-

sus on how the award program will work. Allow approximately 15 minutes for discussion.

Implementation Phase

Implement the award program so that the team member who has demonstrated outstanding performance during the intervening time is acknowledged.

What to Expect

This is a simple activity that provides the team an ongoing means for recognizing the effectiveness of team members. The key to the effectiveness of this activity is the development of a structure that provides for the smooth, credible, and consistent implementation of this award program.

Approximate time: 30-45 minutes (planning phase).

7

Letting Go of Frustrations, Conflicts, and Disappointments

But human existence is half light and half dark,
and our creative possibilities seem strangely linked
to that part of us we keep in the dark.
Trying to bring out our creativity in the workplace,
we suddenly realize how unwelcoming
a professional corporate setting can be
to the darker soul struggles of human existence.
But simply turning away from these shadows,
no matter how professional our environment,
does not mean that they cease to exist.
David Whyte

In the previous chapter on Celebrating, high-performing, spirited teams were characterized by their experience of wonder. Spirited teams, like ordinary teams, must also confront despair. An important difference between spirited teams and ordinary teams is their capacity to embrace the despair, as well as the wonder. Wonder and despair are dimensions of the same reality. When a team opens itself to one, it opens itself to the other. What distinguishes spirited teams from dispirited teams is the capacity to embrace and work with the despair (or dissonance) that develops in team relationships. Working through the despair is facilitated by Letting Go.

Everything in and around the team is full of spirit. Spirited teams learn to discern the spirit in their midst, including the pain of a difficult relationship with a coworker, the missed deadline, the failed experiment, or the breakdown in customer service. By Letting Go and embracing the dissonance the team can cope and transcend its pain—releasing blocked energy. The gift of dissonance is that it offers us a pathway to engage with the team or a team member, to let go of our ego-centered self.

However, all too often embracing the dissonance is displaced by indulging the dissonance. The despair we feel at work perpetuates more despair. When we feel tormented at work, we attract torment. When we are afraid at work, we attract fear.

Letting Go is the capacity to enter into and embrace the shadow—the pain, the despair, the torment, and the fear. Shadow is a Jungian term meaning the part of the self that we keep in the dark, unexplored. Teams, like individuals, put what is unacceptable out of their awareness into the shadow. The possibility of spirit within a team lies in Letting Go, in bringing what is unacceptable into the light and transforming it into useful energy.

Dissonance flourishes in the unconscious. The key to avoiding dissonance is mindfulness—staying conscious of events and persons around us. The first step in Letting Go is becoming conscious about what is going on within the team and within us. The second step is disclosure. Disclosure is deep sharing that allows us to become complete and whole.

Disclosure touches a deep place within. When difficulty occurs in the team we may repress our reactions, perhaps denying the reality of the situation. Healing occurs not in casting out but in embracing the shadow, the dissonance. Team members experiencing the greatest pain, due to a heated conflict with a team member, the ending of a prized career, or the depletion of financial reserves, often report a remarkable quality of spirit residing at the center of this pain. The paradox of life is that getting what is most important often results from Letting Go in the face of fear.

Fear can cause us to try to impose order or control over things and persons that we cannot control. In the grip of fear we try to make things happen, or prevent things from happening, instead of accepting events as they unfold and choosing opportunities that are appropriate to the situation. There is an art to Letting Go of control. This creates space for team members to contribute to each other. Spiritual maturity is a matter of Letting Go of fear, growing in trust, and seeing how we and our needs are being fulfilled through the team.

A certain amount of fear is healthy. For example, we may feel fear in exposing our assumptions and expectations to challenge. Letting Go is the phase of the Team Spirit Spiral that allows us to embrace these challenges.

Through Letting Go we authentically disclose how we feel and what we believe is true. Letting Go is being complete in our communications with coworkers and others. This completion allows freedom in our interactions with team members.

Letting Go also involves giving and receiving constructive feedback that improves relationships that were formerly broken or strained. This requires straight, clear, principled conversations with those on the team with whom we experience dissonance.

Team members may have major obstacles to overcome and can feel victimized by those obstacles. Letting Go suggests that coddling and rescuing such coworkers, however well-intentioned, sells the coworkers short. It suffocates and further immobilizes coworkers. Providing constructive feedback calls them to be their best.

Similarly, feelings of disenchantment with a team member regarding some breakdown in performance call for constructive feedback. Giving constructive feedback requires integrity and commitment. (A process for giving constructive feedback is included in the learning activity, Letting Go through Constructive Feedback.)

Letting Go of fear and making the leap to provide and receive constructive feedback can powerfully transform our lives and energize team performance. Engaging in Letting Go is a great opportunity to continually reframe our relationships, to see things differently, to reframe discouragement into other, more nurturing possibilities.

Team members sometimes mistakenly believe that feelings of anger, disappointment, sadness, or damaged relationships with team members can be reasoned away or ignored. They cannot. By Letting Go we become open to forces within and without ourselves that can provide healing. The learning activities in this chapter encourage the process of Letting Go.

The Learning Activities

Getting Out of the Box allows team members to serve in client and consultant teams for the purpose of generating out-of-the-box thinking that responds to a dissonant team issue.

Letting Go through Constructive Feedback assists team members in developing the skill of giving constructive feedback.

Insights from Athletic, Religious, Entertainment, and World Figures permits team members to have fun acting out the insights of nonbusiness leaders related to some dissonant issue the team is facing.

A Letting Go Ritual engages the team in a debriefing regarding the dissonances that remain after the completion of an important project.

Team Norms encourages team members to apply Letting Go to issues that face the team, developing team norms that will respond to these issues in the future.

Identifying and Responding to Team Dissonances raises critical questions with the team about how best to respond to some dissonant issue.

Dialogue with an Imaginary Guru permits team members to dialogue with a spirit teacher about some vexing issue of Letting Go.

Molding Clay: A Letting Go Metaphor engages team members in working with clay to symbolize the potential for moving an issue from dissonance to consonance.

What to Keep in Mind When Facilitating These Learning Activities

* Support the team in embracing and working through its dissonances.
* Provide constructive feedback and encourage participants to do likewise.
* Disclose what is true for you and encourage participants to do likewise.
* Develop the capacity of the team to work with the dark side (individually and in the team).
* Demonstrate "undefended receptivity"—the capacity to listen to team frustrations and breakdowns.

Learning Goal

To acknowledge dissonances occurring in the team and to provide new perspectives, ideas, and thinking that will allow for moving from dissonance to consonance.

Preparation

1. Photocopy the Nine Dots handout for all participants.
2. Provide four to six plastic storage boxes containing index cards.
3. Tape a blank card with a number (1, 2, 3, etc.) to the top of each box.
4. Create a flip chart display with the heading, Action Steps for Getting Out of the Box.

Note: Because this activity assumes understanding of the Team Spirit Spiral, use one of the following activities from Appendix D as a prelude to this activity: Walk in Nature: Discovering the Phases of the Spiral or The Seasons of a Team's Life: Establishing Team Climate.

Learning Activity

1. Discuss the importance of out-of-the-box thinking to team effectiveness. Explain that an important dimension of Letting Go is the capacity to let go of self-imposed boundaries and rigidities that impede the team's capacity to see things in new ways. Distribute the Nine Dots handout. Determine who in the team is familiar with the nine dot exercise (i.e., the instructions are to connect all nine dots by drawing four unbroken, straight lines). In most groups three-fourths of the participants are familiar with the exercise, but often a majority of those persons cannot remember how to do it. Allow two to three minutes for

team participants to attempt to connect the nine dots, and then ask for a volunteer from the group to share the solution. Stress that the nine dots exercise is a metaphor for the rigidities that exist in teams. Going beyond the nine dots is not always easy for teams or team members. The spaces outside of the nine dots are symbolic of the kind of paradigm-breaking thinking that is characteristic of spirited, high-performing teams.

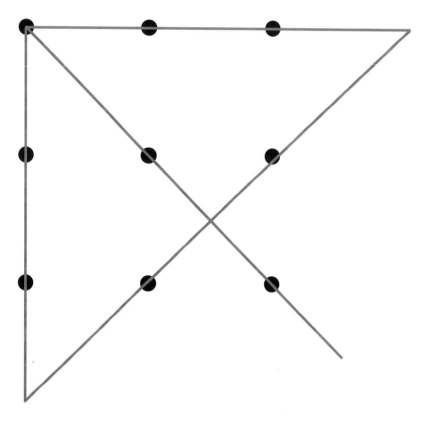

2. Ask team members to identify who they need to be and what they have to do to accomplish out-of-the-box thinking. (Participants typically respond, "high commitment," "ability to accept risk," "challenging," "exciting ways of thinking," etc.) Allow five to ten minutes for discussion.

3. Explain that in this activity team members will work in subteams of two persons, and each subteam will be given a number and a box. Each subteam will begin by being a client team and then will become a consulting team. Each team will have two tasks: a.) Identify a dissonant harmonic from the Team Spirit Spiral experienced by the team; as the client the team will be asking for consultation related to this source of dissonance from the other consulting teams. b.) Provide consultation

regarding the team dissonance presented to your team by other client teams.

4. Direct the teams to choose a dissonance and to describe it with enough detail to give the consulting teams the flavor of the situation.

5. Suggest the following language: "How can we respond to the _____(name the dissonance) when the situation we face is_____?"

   For example, "How can we respond to the <u>withheld communications</u> when the situation we face is <u>our team is dispersed across the U.S. and only comes together six times a year</u>?"

6. Allow 15 minutes for the teams to determine and describe the dissonant factors that they seek to transform into consonant factors.

7. After each team has identified its dissonant factor, they should write a clear description of the dissonance, on the numbered card on the outside of their box.

8. When given the signal to proceed, each team passes its box to another team for consultation. Each team now has five minutes to propose an approach to the resolution of another team's dissonance and record an out-of-the-box idea on one of the cards inside the box, marking their team number on the card.

9. After five minutes the boxes are rotated and the process continues until each team has responded to all the other teams.

10. When all teams have responded to all the boxes, each team has 15 minutes to evaluate the consulting ideas it has received from the other teams and to create a reward for the team offering the best consulting idea.

11. A representative from each team reads the consulting idea that the team evaluated most highly to the whole group and presents the award to the team generating that idea.

12. Ask the full team to identify action steps that it might take to introduce the best consulting ideas into the team's functioning. Allow 20 minutes for this discussion. Record the ideas on the flip chart display you have prepared.

What to Expect

This activity allows the team to do important Letting Go work by identifying a variety of dissonances. It generates useful responses to dissonant factors at work within the team. Emphasize the importance of identifying the concrete circumstances surrounding the dissonant factor in the second part of the sentence that is posted on the box. The key to effective facilitation of the activity is in reinforcing the importance of adhering to the time lines for identifying dissonant elements, as client teams, and of generating pertinent responses, as consulting teams. Create a celebratory mood at the completion of the activity as teams acknowledge consulting ideas and teams. It is important to support the full team in identifying concrete actions for responding to its dissonant elements.

Approximate time: 90-120 minutes.

Note: This activity can be enhanced through the use of the video *Joshua in the Box*. This short, humorous video of a little character called Joshua demonstrates with music and images (no words) the trials and tribulations of being in a box, getting out, and, ultimately, becoming the box. The video can be ordered by contacting CRM Films, 1-800-421-0833. Use this video to elicit discussion about participant interpretations as a prelude to this activity.

Nine Dots

●   ●   ●

●   ●   ●

●   ●   ●

Photocopied from *Building Team Spirit* by Barry Heermann.
Published by McGraw-Hill, ISBN 0-07-028472-5. To order, call 1-800-2MCGRAW.

ACTIVITY

LETTING GO THROUGH CONSTRUCTIVE FEEDBACK

Learning Goal

To develop the skill of using constructive feedback effectively.

Preparation

1. Photocopy the following five handouts for all participants:

> D.A.R.R.N.-It! Continuum
> Letting Go/Constructive Feedback Process
> Roles and Process Activity Form
> Constructive Feedback Planning Form
> Constructive Feedback Observation Form

2. Create a flip chart display with the heading, Letting Go/Constructive Feedback Process, identifying the seven processes listed on the Letting Go/Constructive Feedback Process handout.

Learning Activity

1. Discuss the importance of Letting Go with team participants. Engage the group in a discussion of the value of providing straight, clear feedback to colleagues and peers. Allow approximately 10 minutes for this discussion.

2. Ask each participant to think of a coworker with whom he or she is currently experiencing difficulty. Caution team members that their first instinct will be to "censor out" certain persons because it appears difficult or impossible to communicate with them. Affirm that they should use the safety of this learning activity and the coaching that is available to work with those situations. To help participants choose a coworker,

distribute the D.A.R.R.N.-It! Continuum handout. The D.A.R.R.N.-It! Continuum traces the levels of difficulty that we experience with coworkers, all the way from minor disconnects, to resentment, to resignation. Discuss these levels of interpersonal dissonance with the team, asking them to identify a coworker, peer, supplier, customer, or manager with whom one of these levels of dissonance exists. Recalling such an experience will help ground this learning activity. Allow approximately 10 minutes for this presentation.

3. Suggest that there is a time-proven approach to providing constructive feedback. Describe each of the components of the constructive feedback process, referring to your prepared flip chart display and providing all participants the Letting Go/Constructive Feedback Process handout. Discuss each part of this communication process. When cofacilitating this module you may want to model the process with your partner. If you don't cofacilitate, then generate conversations with team members that reveal the subtleties of effectively providing constructive feedback. Allow approximately 10 minutes for this presentation.

4. This activity will often create dissonance in the room as team members are typically resigned to continued dissonance with others in their life who are "impossible" or "difficult." It is easier for some to live with the resignation than to try to respond. Listen respectfully to what team members have to say and then return them to the process of giving constructive feedback. It is helpful to deepen participants' understanding of resignation, showing how it disempowers them in giving constructive feedback.

5. Here are some important rules of thumb to remember about giving constructive feedback:

   • If you aren't clear about the purpose of your communication, don't give it at all. (Ask team members where most people begin when giving feedback. Typically they will answer with step three, an emotional response. This retort produces resistance or more dissonance. Stress that the key is to operate out of the highest possible sense of purpose with regard to the situation and the person.)

   • Be sure to focus on the facts, situations, issues, or behaviors and not the person or personality (step two).

   • It should not take longer than a minute to get from step one to step four.

6. Ask participants what they might recommend you do if you get to step four and your colleague responds defensively by saying, "I don't see it

that way." This will generate a variety of responses. It is useful to explore responses that are related to the blind spot that the coworker may have about the facts, issues, or behaviors being presented. Because you may be speaking into someone else's blind spot, you may need to recycle steps one through four. Another way to handle such a defensive posture is to ask, "How do you see it?" This requires great discipline in bringing ourselves to fully hearing and understanding the coworker's position. Allow approximately 10 minutes for this discussion.

7. Explain that the team will now enter into the rehearsal component of this activity. Distribute the Roles and Process Activity Form handout. Clarify the triangular relationship between the three key roles: the communicator (the person who will deliver the constructive feedback), the receiver (the person who will perform the role of a real person to whom the communicator would like to deliver constructive feedback), and the observer (a colleague from the team who will take notes and facilitate a feedback session at the completion of the practice). All participants will have a chance to serve in each of the three roles.

8. Ask the team members to clarify in their minds the difficult relationship with a work associate. Remind participants that this dissonant relationship is one that they need to resolve or handle because it is critical to the work of the team or to producing some important team result. Distribute the Constructive Feedback Planning Form handout, and explain the use of the handout. Ask team members to take the time to respond to these questions before beginning the process and to write their responses on the handout, for the person identified earlier.

9. After completing the questions, ask selected team members to share their insights. Ask them to share their intentions for giving constructive feedback as well as the pitfalls in themselves that might confound their effectiveness. Allow approximately ten minutes for completion of the form and a short discussion.

10. Return participants to the Roles and Process Activity Form, clarifying the three phases of the rehearsal. In two minutes the communicator gives the receiver details about the person to whom he or she intends to deliver constructive feedback and states how that person is likely to respond. The second phase is communication of the constructive feedback using the full seven-step process (eight minutes). The third phase, feedback, allows five minutes for the communicator to verbally reflect on what worked and didn't work about the way the constructive feedback was delivered; this is followed by the receiver evaluating what worked and didn't work, followed by the observer, who provides a syn-

thesis, referring to the notes taken on an observation sheet about the communicator's effectiveness. Caution: During the feedback phase the observer will be tempted to respond first. Emphasize that the observers should resist this temptation, allowing the communicator and the receiver the first chance to reflect and respond. Distribute the Constructive Feedback Observation Form, and clarify the use of this form for observers. Ask if there are any questions.

11. Explain that the rehearsal will last about 45 minutes, 15 minutes per round, and that you will be indicating when there are a few minutes left in each 15-minute round. Reinforce the time lines described earlier and stress that the observer should monitor the time. Clarify that each person will have a chance to serve in each of the three roles and that you will be circulating among the rehearsal groups.

12. Determine if there are any questions. Instruct team members to have the seven processes for giving constructive feedback in front of them, as well as their answers to the planning questions and the observation form. Remind observers to write legibly so they can give their written comments to the communicator at the end of each round. Clarify that you will be announcing when they should move from round to round.

13. If there are no further questions, count off and create triads. Ask each triad to go to an area of the room where they will not be disturbed and to choose who will be the communicator, the receiver, and the observer for the first round.

14. Instruct the triads to begin the first round. Carefully monitor time, letting each group know when there are a few minutes remaining so they can complete their feedback. Circulate among the triads throughout each of the three rounds.

15. When all three rounds are completed, debrief the full team. Ask, "What did you see that will contribute to your being effective in giving constructive feedback? What worked? What didn't work?"

What to Expect

This Letting Go exercise provides valuable skill development in giving constructive feedback. It is organized into two parts: a didactic component that engages participants in a discussion of the challenge and value of giving constructive feedback and a skill-building component. Because of the high level of resignation that some team members experience with colleagues, this activity usefully, and sometimes uncomfortably, challenges the resistance that inhibits team members from entering into constructive feedback conversations. Participants will gain most by focusing this activity on an actual experience with a coworker in the organization.

Excellent facilitation of this module will deepen awareness of the challenges and opportunities for giving constructive feedback. It is important that the ground rules for giving constructive feedback are reinforced, as suggested in item five. Because some participants will perceive the constructive feedback process as too Pollyannaish, it is important that the facilitator pick up on this energy, displaying the dissonant response of a hypothetical receiver, and taking a purposely resistant attitude toward the feedback, as suggested in item six.

The key to effective facilitation of the skill component is crisp, clear explanation of the rehearsal, including:

the three rehearsal roles,

the requirements of each rehearsal phase,

the timing of each rehearsal phase, and

the handouts used in conjunction with the rehearsal.

It is useful to repeat these parameters for the rehearsal, asking if team participants have questions.

Facilitation of the discussion following the skill component provides the opportunity for team members to share their experience and, critically, to acknowledge the importance of using constructive feedback. The importance of using this Letting Go skill can prompt team members to suggest that the team develop a norm for consistently using this skill to handle its difficult communications. Should this come up, facilitate the discussion and help the team come to consensus about this suggestion.

Approximate time: 100-150 minutes.

Attitudes that we develop about colleagues disempower us and the team. These attitudes lead to dispirited relationships. Seize the moment: Notice when you are beginning to feel disconnected from a coworker and provide constructive feedback or get coaching.

Disconnection: We begin to feel a little removed and at odds with our colleague(s).

Antagonism: We begin to feel dissonance with our colleague(s).

Resentment: We begin to feel anger or bitterness toward our colleague(s), blaming them for the situation.

Resignation: We feel resigned about the colleague(s), selling out on them and, critically, on ourselves (i.e., there isn't anything we could or would do about it.).

Numbness: We repress our feelings, going numb.

Photocopied from *Building Team Spirit* by Barry Heermann.
Published by McGraw-Hill, ISBN 0-07-028472-5. To order, call 1-800-2MCGRAW.

Letting Go/Constructive Feedback Process

1. Describe the purpose of your feedback.

2. Provide your observations of the relevant facts, issues, situations, and behaviors.

3. Describe your reactions.

4. Invite a response from this individual.

5. State your understanding of what you are hearing.

6. Together, create new ways to proceed and reach agreement about what to do.

7. Plan next steps and offer your support.

Photocopied from *Building Team Spirit* by Barry Heermann.
Published by McGraw-Hill, ISBN 0-07-028472-5. To order, call 1-800-2MCGRAW.

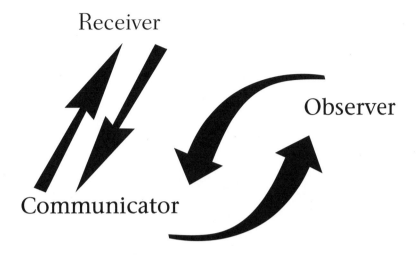

	Phase 1 Preparation 2 minutes	Phase 2 Communication 8 minutes	Phase 3 Feedback 5 minutes
Communicator			
Receiver			
Observer			

Photocopied from *Building Team Spirit* by Barry Heermann.
Published by McGraw-Hill, ISBN 0-07-028472-5. To order, call 1-800-2MCGRAW.

Constructive Feedback Planning Form

1. What is your goal in providing constructive feedback to this work associate?

   _____

   _____

   _____

   _____

   _____

   _____

   _____

   _____

   _____

2. What are the relevant facts, issues, situations, and behaviors?

   _____

   _____

   _____

   _____

   _____

   _____

   _____

   _____

   _____

3. What are your reactions/feelings/responses?

   _____

   _____

   _____

   _____

   _____

   _____

   _____

   _____

   _____

Photocopied from *Building Team Spirit* by Barry Heermann.
Published by McGraw-Hill, ISBN 0-07-028472-5. To order, call 1-800-2MCGRAW.

4. What suggestions might you offer to, or what requests might you make of, this individual that would result in a refocusing of his or her energy?

_____

_____

_____

_____

_____

_____

_____

_____

_____

_____

_____

_____

5. What do you need to be mindful of about yourself in order to make a difference with this individual?

_____

_____

_____

_____

_____

_____

_____

_____

_____

_____

_____

Photocopied from *Building Team Spirit* by Barry Heermann.
Published by McGraw-Hill, ISBN 0-07-028472-5. To order, call 1-800-2MCGRAW.

Constructive Feedback Observation Form

1. Did the communicator effectively describe the purpose of his or her feedback?

   _____

   _____

   _____

   _____

   _____

   _____

   _____

   _____

2. Did the communicator provide observations of the relevant facts, issues, situations, and behaviors?

   _____

   _____

   _____

   _____

   _____

   _____

   _____

   _____

3. Did the communicator describe his or her reactions?

   _____

   _____

   _____

   _____

   _____

   _____

   _____

   _____

Photocopied from *Building Team Spirit* by Barry Heermann.
Published by McGraw-Hill, ISBN 0-07-028472-5. To order, call 1-800-2MCGRAW.

4. Did the communicator invite a response from the receiver?

_____

_____

_____

_____

_____

_____

5. Did the communicator state his or her understanding of what the receiver was saying?

_____

_____

_____

_____

_____

_____

6. Did the communicator establish a way to proceed and reach some agreement with the receiver?

_____

_____

_____

_____

_____

7. Did the communicator offer next steps and support?

_____

_____

_____

_____

_____

_____

Photocopied from *Building Team Spirit* by Barry Heermann.
Published by McGraw-Hill, ISBN 0-07-028472-5. To order, call 1-800-2MCGRAW.

Learning Goals

1. To acknowledge the dissonant factors that inhibit the work of the team.
2. To generate new perspectives and to design action steps that respond to the dissonance.

Preparation

1. Provide a basket or other container, roughly 10" in diameter, to hold a half-dozen 3 x 5 cards.
2. Provide notepaper for all participants.
3. Photocopy the Team Spirit Harmonics handout for all participants.
4. Create three flip chart displays with the headings:

> Key Dissonant Factors
>
> Promising Ideas from Prominent Figures
>
> Action Steps.

Note: Because this activity assumes understanding of the Team Spirit Spiral, use one of the following activities from Appendix D as a prelude to this activity: Walk in Nature: Discovering the Phases of the Spiral or The Seasons of a Team's Life: Establishing Team Climate.

Learning Activity

1. Explain that in this activity the team will explore the most debilitating dissonant factors that affect their performance and relationships. To accomplish this, ask the team to think through each of the phases of the Team Spirit Spiral and consider all dissonant possibilities. Distribute the Team Spirit Harmonics handout, so that participants can scan the dissonant factors related to each phase of the Spiral. Ask the team to begin

brainstorming dissonances they experience in the team, whether small or large. Record the dissonant factors on the first flip chart display. Allow 15 to 30 minutes for this brainstorming.

2. Ask the team to prioritize the dissonant factors. (It may make sense to combine several dissonant factors into a single category.) Request that the team identify a single dissonance that they would like to address first as a team.

3. After identifying the dissonant factor, ask the team to provide several concrete examples of how this dissonance operates within and impedes the team. Steer the team away from abstractions and return them to concrete examples.

4. Having identified the dissonance and how it manifests itself in concrete terms, suggest that what is needed is fresh insight about how to respond to this team dissonance. Ask the team to suspend consideration of the dissonance for the time being and instead focus their attention on famous persons in nonbusiness realms, such as politics, sports, music, theater, religion, etc. Ask that they agree upon six well known figures who they can associate with the six phases of the Team Spirit Spiral. For example, identify and agree upon a prominent figure who is especially gifted at Initiating (i.e., creating relationship, trust, and belonging). After identifying that figure, go on to identify a prominent person who is adept at Visioning, and so on through Service. The team must reach consensus on each person. As a prominent figure is identified, write the phase of the Spiral and the person's name on one of the 3 x 5 cards. Allow approximately 20 to 40 minutes for the team to identify these prominent personalities.

5. Ask the team to divide into six groups. Each group will be assigned a phase of the Spiral and the accompanying prominent figure. (In teams smaller than six persons, one person may need to take more than one phase.) Ask team members to draw the names and related phases from the basket. After all cards have been drawn, ask team members to explore the dissonant factor from the unique perspective of the prominent figure they have drawn. Allow team members 10 to 15 minutes to reflect on and take notes regarding the insights that their prominent figure would offer, using the notepaper provided.

6. When all team members have completed their reflection and notes, ask for a spokesperson from each group to present the insights of the prominent person. Request that presentations be limited to five minutes each. Ask for a volunteer to begin the presentations; it is not essential that the phases of the Spiral be explored in sequence. After each presentation ask

the team what they learned that might be applied to the dissonance they face. Record their ideas on the second flip chart display. Allow approximately 30 to 50 minutes for presentations and distilling implications for the team.

7. After recording all of the ideas that were generated based upon the presentations of the prominent figures, ask the team to identify the most promising ideas. Request that they translate these most promising ideas into action steps that might be taken to move their dissonance to a consonance. Record their ideas on the third flip chart display.

What to Expect

This is a fun activity that provides a different perspective on Letting Go as a result of the consulting ideas from prominent figures. The team will enjoy selecting these personalities and interpreting their thoughts regarding the issue. Successful facilitation of this activity depends on attention to two areas: first, moving the team from identification of dissonant factors and prominent figures through the presentation of the thinking of prominent figures regarding a key dissonance; and second, helping the team to identify the most promising ideas, formulating them as action steps.

Approximate time: 120-150 minutes.

CONSONANCES

(a combination of musical tones that have resolved—that is, they are in agreement)

Service
-*contribution*: generously and freely giving to another
-*aligned execution*: fulfilling, in a unified way, customer and team needs
-*mutual support*: providing reciprocal assistance

Initiating
-*orientation*: becoming familiarized and aware
-*belonging*: feeling allied with and a part of the team
-*trust*: feeling reliant and secure about team members

Visioning
-*shared vision/values*: agreeing on what is possible and its underlying worth and merit
-*compassion*: experiencing empathy and concern for another
-*presence*: deeply experiencing the purpose of the team

Claiming
-*goal/role alignment*: agreeing on the outcome and the means for achieving it
-*organization support*: securing the necessary resources from the organization
-*competence*: developing skills and awareness needed to perform team roles

Celebrating
-*appreciation*: feeling recognized and acknowledged
-*energy*: experiencing vitality and aliveness
-*wonder*: experiencing an unbounded sense of possibility

Letting Go
-*disclosure*: revealing previously suppressed attitudes and opinions
-*constructive feedback*: providing forthright responses that encourage growth
—*completion*: feeling a sense of freedom when everything has been said

DISSONANCES

(a combination of unresolved musical tones)

Service
-*depletion*: feeling used up, unable to freely give to another
-*uncoordinated action*: incompletely fulfilling customer and team needs
-*unsupportiveness*: acting without concern for others

Initiating
-*disorientation*: experiencing disequilibrium and fear
-*alienation*: feeling like a misfit, not a part of the team
-*mistrust*: feeling insecure and cautious about team members

Visioning
-*ambiguous vision/values*: experiencing uncertainty about what is possible—let alone its underlying worth and merit
-*callousness*: being insensitive and harsh
-*aridness*: feeling barren and empty, without a sense of purpose

Claiming
-*nonalignment*: disagreeing about the outcome and means for achieving it
-*nonsupport*: being unable to secure the necessary resources from the organization
-*deficiency*: not having the skills and awareness needed to perform team roles

Celebrating
-*nonappreciation*: not feeling recognized and acknowledged
-*burnout*: feeling used up and ineffective in the team
-*disenchantment*: feeling repelled and put out

Letting Go
-*withheld communication*: concealing attitudes and opinions from others
-*criticism*: offering unsupportive critical feedback
-*incompletion*: feeling regretful about withholding communications

Photocopied from *Building Team Spirit* by Barry Heermann.
Published by McGraw-Hill, ISBN 0-07-028472-5. To order, call 1-800-2MCGRAW.

A LETTING GO RITUAL

Learning Goal

To learn how to take time to formally end and let go of the team's disappointments, fears, discouragements, etc., through a Letting Go ritual.

Preparation

1. Provide a heavy pottery pot, large ashtray, or bowl containing sand.
2. Provide slips of notepaper for all team members.
3. Make matches or a candle available.

Learning Activity

1. On the slips of notepaper provided, direct team members to write the names of persons, situations, issues, etc. that they would like to let go of, to symbolically bring closure to a project they worked on together. Allow approximately 15 minutes for identifying and writing.
2. Ask team members to step forward to the vessel one by one, light their pieces of notepaper, and express aloud—if they are willing—the area of completion and their reaction to symbolically bringing closure to this area of their work. Allow approximately 15 minutes for burning and individual expressions of Letting Go.
3. After all team members have stepped forward to burn and let go of their issues, ask members to share their reaction to the experience with a partner, detailing any steps that may still need to be taken to bring full closure. Allow approximately 8 minutes for sharing in pairs.
4. Ask the full team to share any additional reflections regarding this learning activity.

What to Expect

Participants experience a release from Letting Go of those persons, situations, issues, etc., that have generated dissonance. This is an excellent activity to use at the completion of a project or major task.

Approximate time: 40-60 minutes.

ACTIVITY

TEAM NORMS

Learning Goals

1. To acknowledge group behaviors or norms that create dissonance in the team.
2. To change those behaviors or norms to increase the team's effectiveness.

Preparation

Create two flip chart displays with the headings, Counterproductive Behaviors and Group Norms.

Learning Activity

1. Begin by asking the group to identify those counterproductive behaviors, impediments, and roadblocks to team effectiveness that team members unwittingly instigate. Record responses on the first flip chart display. Allow approximately 15 to 20 minutes for generating a list of counterproductive behaviors.

2. Ask team members to generate group norms that will respond to these barriers and improve team functioning. Team-generated norms might address interruptions at meetings, missed meetings, missed deadlines, gossip, passing the buck or insensitive remarks that diminish trust. Record ideas generated on the second flip chart display. Examples of norms might include starting and stopping meetings on time and providing constructive feedback to each other. Allow approximately 15 minutes for identifying group norms.

3. Ask the group to respond to the list of group norms it generated. Is there a consensus among the group that these norms will help to improve the spirit of the team? Are there norms that still need to be added?

4. Ask if any team members would like to select one of the norms to safe-guard. Identify a specific norm that might be challenging for the team and ask for a commitment to try it out in the team for a specified period of time (e.g., two weeks) and then evaluate its usefulness.

What to Expect

This is a great activity to use with teams that have not developed group norms or that are experiencing dissonance in their meetings or work together. Successful facilitation involves getting the team to disclose all of its dissonant factors and to identify and reach consensus on team norms that would respond to those dissonant factors. A critical team evaluation at the end of each meeting that addresses whether the norms were observed can be very helpful. This activity is also useful to start-up teams working through Initiating issues.

Approximate time: 45-60 minutes.

ACTIVITY
IDENTIFYING AND RESPONDING TO
TEAM DISSONANCES

Learning Goals

1. To identify an area of team dissonance.
2. To develop action steps to respond to the dissonance.

Preparation

1. Photocopy the Dissonance Check Sheet handout for all participants.
2. Create two flip chart displays with the headings, Most Dissonant Factors Facing Team and Action Steps.
3. Photocopy the Key Questions Regarding the Dissonant Factor handout for all participants.

Learning Activity

1. Distribute the Dissonance Check Sheet handout. Request that participants identify the six most serious dissonances that they believe the team is facing, organizing them in order of priority concern. Allow five to ten minutes for participants to make their choices.
2. Ask volunteers to share their most dissonant factors. Involve all participants. Record responses on the flip chart display. Work to achieve consensus about which dissonant factor or combination of factors most debilitates the team. Allow 15 to 30 minutes for this discussion.
3. When the most critical dissonant factor or combination of dissonant factors has been identified, request that participants work individually in response to a series of questions regarding this dissonance. Distribute the Key Questions Regarding the Dissonant Factor handout. These questions are designed to generate new perspective about how the team

might respond. Allow 15 to 20 minutes for participants to respond to the questions.

4. When all participants have completed their responses, ask individuals to share their insights. Suggest that these insights be stated as action steps that might be taken in response to the dissonance. Record the responses on the flip chart display. Allow 15 to 20 minutes for generating action steps.

5. Ask the team to identify changes in thinking that have occurred as a result of completing this learning activity.

What to Expect

This activity uses a methodical approach to identifying and examining team dissonance. For many teams the exploration and open analysis of dissonance serves to clear the air and move the team forward. The value of this activity is in understanding and working with the dissonance, rather than ignoring it, including designing action steps that specifically respond to the dissonance.

Approximate time: 60-90 minutes.

Identify the six most serious dissonances that you believe the team is facing, organizing them in order of priority concern (1 being the highest concern, 2 the next highest, etc.).

1. **Service**
   ____ depletion
   ____ uncoordinated action
   ____ unsupportiveness

2. **Initiating**
   ____ disorientation
   ____ alienation
   ____ mistrust

3. **Visioning**
   ____ ambiguous vision/values
   ____ callousness
   ____ aridness

4. **Claiming**
   ____ nonalignment
   ____ nonsupport (organization)
   ____ deficiency

5. **Celebrating**
   ____ nonappreciation
   ____ burnout
   ____ disenchantment

6. **Letting Go**
   ____ withheld communications
   ____ criticism
   ____ incompletion

Photocopied from *Building Team Spirit* by Barry Heermann.
Published by McGraw-Hill, ISBN 0-07-028472-5. To order, call 1-800-2MCGRAW.

1. What dissonant factor most interferes with the work of the team?

   _____

   _____

2. What reasons can you see for the current dissonance being so disruptive to the team?

   _____

   _____

3. How long has this dissonance been developing?

   _____

   _____

4. In what ways has the team been avoiding the dissonance?

   _____

   _____

5. What do you know intuitively about this situation?

   _____

   _____

6. How are you willing to facilitate movement through the dissonance?

   _____

   _____

7. What new order is emerging out of the dissonance?

   _____

   _____

8. What is this situation teaching you, personally?

   _____

   _____

9. What is this situation teaching the team?

   _____

   _____

10. What new spirit on the team can you imagine coming out of successfully working through this dissonance?

    _____

    _____

Photocopied from *Building Team Spirit* by Barry Heermann.
Published by McGraw-Hill, ISBN 0-07-028472-5. To order, call 1-800-2MCGRAW.

ACTIVITY

DIALOGUE WITH AN IMAGINARY GURU

Learning Goals

To gain insight on how to handle a dissonant work relationship by having an imaginary dialogue with a valued friend, colleague, teacher, or family member.

Preparation

1. Photocopy the D.A.R.R.N.-It! Continuum for all participants.
2. Photo copy the Dialogue handout for all participants.

Learning Activity

1. Suggest to participants that it is natural for many team members to experience dissonances with team or organizational colleagues. These dissonances may take the form of minor personal disconnects all the way to resentment and resignation that diminish and sometimes prohibit the relationship. Distribute the D.A.R.R.N.-It! Continuum handout. Review each of the levels of the continuum, asking for reflections from team members about when they have observed these levels in this and other organizations. Allow 15 to 20 minutes for this discussion.
2. Request that team participants identify and record on the Dialogue handout provided someone with whom they currently feel some level of dissonance in some domain of their work relationships: a peer, a manager, a supplier, a team colleague, a customer, etc. Ask them to identify this person and spend a few minutes reflecting on the facts and issues surrounding the dissonant relationship. Allow 10 to 20 minutes for reflection and writing using the dialogue handout.
3. For the next few minutes, ask participants to put aside the person and situation that they identified. Ask that they now identify a valued friend,

colleague, or teacher—an imaginary guru—who might help them gain insight about this dissonant relationship. Allow five minutes for participants to identify their imaginary gurus.

4. On the Dialogue handout, ask participants to enter into a written, imaginary dialogue with their valued friend or associate about this dissonant relationship, moving back and forth between the two columns. (The first column is for the participant and the second column is for the imaginary guru). Allow approximately 15 minutes.

5. When all dialogues have been completed ask participants to share their new insights about the dissonant relationship. In closing, ask what participants have observed as a result of this learning activity.

What to Expect

This activity provides a safe environment for individual team members to explore alternative ways to respond to a dissonant relationship. Participants may choose to share or not share their insights. Beneficial dialogues can come from this activity on how best to respond to difficult situations, whether or not participants choose to disclose any of the specifics of their situation.

Approximate time: 60-90 minutes.

D.A.R.R.N.-It! Continuum

Attitudes that we develop about colleagues disempower us and the team. These attitudes lead to dispirited relationships. Seize the moment: Notice when you are beginning to feel disconnected from a coworker and provide constructive feedback or get coaching.

Disconnection: We begin to feel a little removed and at odds with our colleague(s).

Antagonism: We begin to feel dissonance with our colleague(s).

Resentment: We begin to feel anger or bitterness toward our colleague(s), blaming them for the situation.

Resignation: We feel resigned about the colleague(s), selling out on them and, critically, on ourselves (i.e., there isn't anything we could or would do about it.).

Numbness: We repress our feelings, going numb.

Photocopied from *Building Team Spirit* by Barry Heermann.
Published by McGraw-Hill, ISBN 0-07-028472-5. To order, call 1-800-2MCGRAW.

1. Person who I currently feel some level of dissonance with in some area of work relationship (peer, manager, supplier, team colleague, customer, etc.):

   _____

2. The facts and issues surrounding the dissonant relationship:

   _____
   _____
   _____
   _____

3. A valued friend, colleague, teacher—an imaginary guru—who might help me gain insight about this dissonant relationship:

   _____

4. Dialogue with this imaginary guru, moving back and forth between the columns in dialogue about this dissonant relationship.

   My comments: My imaginary guru's comments:

   _____   _____
   _____   _____
   _____   _____
   _____   _____
   _____   _____
   _____   _____
   _____   _____
   _____   _____
   _____   _____
   _____   _____
   _____   _____
   _____   _____

Photocopied from Building Team Spirit by Barry Heermann.
Published by McGraw-Hill, ISBN 0-07-028472-5. To order, call 1-800-2MCGRAW.

My comments (continued):

_____
_____
_____
_____
_____
_____
_____
_____
_____
_____
_____
_____
_____
_____
_____
_____
_____
_____
_____
_____
_____
_____
_____
_____
_____

My imaginary guru's comments (continued):

_____
_____
_____
_____
_____
_____
_____
_____
_____
_____
_____
_____
_____
_____
_____
_____
_____
_____
_____
_____
_____
_____
_____
_____
_____

Photocopied from *Building Team Spirit* by Barry Heermann.
Published by McGraw-Hill, ISBN 0-07-028472-5. To order, call 1-800-2MCGRAW.

MOLDING CLAY: A LETTING GO METAPHOR

Learning Goal

To work with molding clay to move beyond and transform a painful or difficult experience, enhancing individual and team effectiveness.

Preparation

1. Provide each member of the team with Play-Doh® or clay.
2. Provide newspaper to cover the tables and damp cloths for cleanup.
3. Provide notepaper for all participants.

Learning Activity

1. Ask the team members to think about some dissonance within the organization or team that keeps them from performing at their highest level. Ask them to express this in a metaphoric shape using the clay. Allow approximately 15 minutes for shaping the clay.
2. Ask them to use the same clay to create another metaphor for how things might be different—that is, the consonant form of the dissonance identified in the first clay image. What does their metaphor symbolize? Allow approximately 15 minutes for molding this second clay image.
3. After completion, ask team members to reflect in writing their observations about what the two metaphors teach them about the dissonance they experience and the consonance they wish to create. Did the process of creating with the clay provide new insights? Allow approximately 10 minutes for reflection and writing.
4. Request that team members share their metaphors with the group, displaying the completed "consonance model."
5. After all members have shared, ask the group to discuss what they have learned.

What to Expect

This activity changes the pace and modality from other activities in this series, and participants enjoy the experience. The use of clay allows participants to tap into a different level of understanding. Part of the usefulness of this activity is eliciting the insights at the completion of the activity that team participants observed about their Letting Go issue.

Approximate time: 60 minutes.

8

Serving Customers and Teams

*Everyone has a purpose in life...a unique gift
or special talent to give to others.
And when we blend this unique talent with service to others,
we experience the ecstasy and exultation of our own spirit,
which is the ultimate goal of all goals.*
Deepak Chopra

The ultimate measure of a spirited, high-performing team is Service. Service emerges powerfully in great teams. It is as if the soul of the team leaps up and declares "This is **it**! This is what we will take on. We will not let another day pass without bringing our full passion to contributing in this way."

Spirited teams provide Service *to* customers and to the team. Think of the blades of a pair of shears: One blade is Service to customers, and the other is Service to the team. They cut best when they are in direct contact with each other. In some organizations, Service is provided at yet another level, to the community and the planet ... like Ben and Jerry's Ice Cream, Anita Roddick's The Body Shop, and Tom's of Maine.

Spirited teams provide Service *through* the energies of the team. The energy of the team exceeds the sum of individual energies present in the team. The drive to serve operating within individuals is integral to the Service provided by the team.

Individuals have unique spirits that give rise to their being and action in the world. Similarly, every team has a unique spirit. Service is an expression of this inner essence or spirit. Spirit is the bridge between resources and results. It is spirit that transforms energy into Service. All the work of the team converges around Service.

The key to great Service is listening at a deep level to colleagues and customers. Brilliant Service also requires a special kind of deep listening within ourselves, to an inner knowing (or intuition). We need to be very quiet to do this. Intuitive listening leads to awareness of our unique contribution or "spirit of Service." Achieving awareness of "spirit of Service" guides us effortlessly and joyously to the use of undiscovered skills, capacities, resources, and talents. Similarly, teams must enter into this inquiry to discover their "spirit of Service."

Spirited teams provide an awakening for members who have not yet discovered their inner essence and talents. The extraordinary contributions of these teams fosters appreciation for the possibility of individual and team greatness and potential to serve.

Albert North Whitehead, the British philosopher, suggests that learning occurs in three distinct phases. Substituting "Service" for "learning" suggests something of how Service evolves for individuals and teams over time.

- The first phase is *emotion*: This is the initial encounter with some reality and as a result of it our hearts are awakened. The encounter touches something inside us that delights and influences our innermost self.

- The second phase is *precision*: This is the rigor and discipline that we bring to Service.

- The third phase is *generalization*: This integrates the deep emotional spark of the first phase with the discipline and thoughtful attention of the second phase at a whole new level of professionalism and distinguished contribution.

It is pleasurable to feel one has something of value to offer; it is pleasurable to receive something of value. Service is the act of giving and receiving, exchanging basic life commodities created by energy and intention. It is the ultimate expression of what it is to be a human being, and it is the ultimate expression of *Building Team Spirit*. During the final days of Abraham Maslow's life he acknowledged that the zenith of human life is not self-actualization, but rather self-transcendence and Service.

The impediments to Service are fear, hurt, and doubt about ourselves and about others (the team, the organization), or about the nature of our work. When we are impeded we perceive others as objects and we concentrate on our own needs. Service burns dimly for these individuals and teams, and suffering becomes a defining characteristic of the team's culture. The absence of Letting Go and Celebrating in team life are clues that fear, hurt, and self-doubt are empowered within the team and need to be responded to.

It is important to acknowledge that individuals new to a team have levels of fear, hurt, and self-doubt as a result of childhood woundedness and unsatisfactory encounters in past teams and organizations. Suffering is present in all human life, and the Initiating phase of the Team Spirit Spiral acknowledges these feelings. Spirited teams give skillful attention to Initiating and Visioning, transforming their members. Spirited teams transform not only team members but also customers and community.

The Learning Activities

Service Circle invites team members to identify with ideas of Service expressed by international figures known for their contribution and Service.

Symbolizing Service allows team members to deepen their awareness of Service by choosing something that symbolizes Service for them.

Meeting Your Inner Servant invites team members to participate in a guided visualization to gain insights about Service.

Revealing the Spirit of Service—Individual and **Revealing the Spirit of Service—Team** provide individual team members and teams with a process for identifying their "spirit of Service" from which greatness arises.

The Keys to the Kingdom encourages team participants to interpret archetypes for Service and a key phase of the Spiral that is instrumental to their providing brilliant Service.

Finding the Ground the Team Stands On supports team members in integrating outer expressions of Service (e.g., products) with inner expressions of Service (e.g., the underlying meaning and purpose—spirit—that impels the team).

Miracle Worker provides a communication structure in which team members interact with customers to better support customer Service.

Archetypes for Service gives team members an opportunity to choose symbols that express the spirit of Service in the team.

What to Keep in Mind When Facilitating These Learning Activities

- Support team members in "connecting" at a deep level regarding their work.
- Assist team members in supporting each other in delivering Service.
- Help team members align their energies to best serve Customers.

• Help team members to explore the nature and essence of contribution that most matters to them and their customers.
• Help the team connect to its spirit of Service.

Learning Goal

To provide an opportunity for team members to experience various perspectives on Service from the point of view of international figures respected for their contributions.

Preparation

1. Photocopy each of the handouts in the series, Perspectives on Service. Create a separate, smaller handout, cutting out the five quotes on each page, and laminating each quote in plastic. Place the quotes on a table in front of the room. Note: Each quote in the series is from a world leader on Service. These quotes were taken from a poster, with accompanying photographs of world leaders, created and disseminated by the Caring Institute. As an alternative to using the handouts, the poster, called "In Search of Secrets from the Universe," may be ordered by writing to The Caring Institute, 519 C Street, NE, Washington, D.C. 20002-5809, or by calling 202-547-4273. The cost is $5 plus shipping and handling. The photograph of each world leader and its accompanying quote can be cut out separately and laminated.

2. Be thoughtful about the layout of the room, because the group will need space to create an inner and an outer circle after completing the written part of the activity.

3. Provide notepaper for all participants.

4. Create a flip chart display with the heading, Insights about Service.

Learning Activity

1. Place one set of the Perspectives on Service handouts or the laminated cards with quotes from prominent world leaders on a table in front of the

room, inviting participants to gather around the table to select their favorite quotes. (See item 1 under Preparation for clarification of these options.)

2. Ask participants to take their quotes and return to their spaces around a U-shaped table. On the notepaper provided, ask participants to write down their thoughts on the quote they chose and why it speaks to them about Service. Allow five minutes.

3. Divide the group into an inner and an outer circle, with each team member paired and facing another team member. (If the group is not an even-numbered team, you or your cofacilitator should join the group.)

4. Each team member has two minutes to clearly express his or her reasons for choosing a person and a quote on Service to his or her partner.

5. Indicate when the two-minute interval is up and give the other partners two minutes to share.

6. After both partners have shared, have the inner circle move one person to the left and begin the two-minute sharing with new partners.

7. Continue this movement to the left for two more rounds.

8. Adapt as needed for smaller or larger groups.

9. Reconvene the team around the table. Have the participants share any new awareness from this experience.

10. Ask team members if their thinking about Service changed as they moved around the circle. Determine if what they heard from others influenced what they said or how they responded to the next person. Ask participants what other awareness they developed from participating in this exercise. Record insights about Service on the flip chart you have prepared.

11. Ask team members to consider the specific business realities of their insights regarding this activity. Ask the team to consider these reflections on Service as it has to do with the team's mission and purpose.

What to Expect

Participants enjoy choosing from among these quotes. They sometimes identify with a figure's sense of Service, and they enjoy sharing a figure and a quote with colleagues. A key to successfully facilitating this activity is to have participants share what they learned about Service from it.

Approximate time: 60 minutes.

"Only a life lived for others is a life worthwhile."

Albert Einstein (20th-Century Scientist)

"We make a living by what we get.
We make a life by what we give."

Sir Winston Churchill (England's Prime Minister during WW II)

"When one reaches out to help another
he touches the face of God."

Walt Whitman (American Poet, Writer)

"You have to be honest with people.
You have to have great respect for yourself.
If you see something that is not right,
you must do something about it."

Annie Wauneka (Freedom Award Winner for Navajo Indian Health Initiatives)

"Progress comes from caring more about what
needs to be done than about who gets the credit."

Dorothy Height (Past President of National Council of Negro Women)

"The greatest source of happiness is forgetting
yourself and trying seriously
and honestly to be useful to others."

Millicent Fenwick (Former Republican Congresswoman Committed to Human Rights)

"Great men are they who see that
the spiritual is stronger than any material force
and that thought rules the world."

Ralph Waldo Emerson (Essayist, Poet)

"Life's most persistent and urgent question is:
'What are you doing for others?'"

Martin Luther King, Jr. (Civil Rights Leader)

"Each of us has within us
a Mother Theresa and a Hitler.
It is up to us to choose what we want to be."

Elisabeth Kübler-Ross (Death and Dying Authority)

"Nothing we do ever stands by itself. If it is good,
it will serve some good purpose in the future.
If it is evil, it may haunt us and
handicap our efforts in unimagined ways."

Eleanor Roosevelt (Humanitarian, U.S. Ambassador to UN)

Photocopied from *Building Team Spirit* by Barry Heermann.
Published by McGraw-Hill, ISBN 0-07-028472-5. To order, call 1-800-2MCGRAW.

"We can only survive when we have
a goal—a passionate
purpose which bears upon the public interest."

Margaret E. Kuhn (Founder of the Grey Panthers)

"I will unite with anyone to do good,
but with no one to do harm."

Frederick Douglass (Abolitionist, Orator, Journalist)

"There is joy in transcending self to serve others."

Mother Theresa (Humanitarian, Nobel Peace Prize Recipient)

"There is a land of the living and a land of the dead;
the bridge is love,
the only survival, the only meaning."

Thornton Wilder (Novelist and Playwright)

"What is important is that one be capable of love.
It is perhaps the only glimpse that we are permitted
of eternity."

Helen Hayes (First Lady of the American Stage)

Photocopied from *Building Team Spirit* by Barry Heermann.
Published by McGraw-Hill, ISBN 0-07-028472-5. To order, call 1-800-2MCGRAW.

"Have I done any good in the world today? Have I cheered up the sad and made someone feel glad? If not I have failed indeed."

Ester Peterson (Assistant Secretary of Labor, Kennedy Administration)

"There is a destiny that makes us brothers. No one goes his way alone. What we send into the lives of others comes back into our own."

Edwin Markham (Poet, Lecturer, called "Dean of American Poetry")

Love is the ultimate and highest goal to which one can aspire. The salvation of humanity is through love and in love."

Viktor Frankl (Holocaust Survivor, Author of *Man's Search for Meaning*)

"Whether for the individual or for the nation, self is best served by transcending self."

Senator Frank E. Moss (Former Republican Senator from Utah)

"So many gods, so many creeds, so many paths... while just the art of being kind is all the world needs."

Ella Wheeler Wilcox (18th-Century Writer of Inspirational Verse)

Photocopied from *Building Team Spirit* by Barry Heermann.
Published by McGraw-Hill, ISBN 0-07-028472-5. To order, call 1-800-2MCGRAW.

Learning Goal

To explore the meaning of Service by identifying a symbol that personalizes the individual beliefs, values, and meaning that participants attach to Service.

Preparation

1. Arrange for a training site that is accessible to an outdoor, pastoral, natural setting, where team members are permitted to walk and explore.
2. Photocopy the Service: What Is It? handout for all participants.

Learning Activity

1. Briefly address the importance of Service to team effectiveness. Ask participants to think about the concept of Service and what it means to them with regard to serving their team, serving customers, and serving the community.
2. Distribute the Service: What Is It? handout. Request that participants record their answers to the first question. Allow approximately five minutes.
3. Instruct participants to look for an object in the natural environment adjacent to the training site that symbolizes the essence of Service. Allow approximately 20 to 30 minutes for participants to go outdoors and find their symbols of Service.
4. After all team members have returned, have them place their symbols on the table in front of them. Request that participants quietly concentrate on their objects, considering what their symbols teach them about

Service. After having reflected on their symbols, ask participants to return to the Service: What Is It? handout and respond to the second question. Allow five minutes for this reflection and writing.

5. After recording their reflections, have participants share their objects and experiences with the group. For a team of ten, allow approximately 20 minutes for sharing.

What to Expect

Participants are able to express metaphorically a new understanding of Service by participating in this activity. The reports of participants are often moving accounts of how Service is present in their lives and work.

Approximate time: 60 minutes.

Team Member Handout

Service: What Is It?

1. In the space below record thoughts that come to mind about what Service means to you and what it means to be a servant of others—a team, a customer, or a community:

_____
_____
_____
_____
_____
_____
_____
_____
_____
_____
_____
_____
_____
_____
_____

2. Reflect on what your symbol of Service teaches you about Service, and record your thoughts and impressions in the space below:

_____
_____
_____
_____
_____
_____
_____
_____
_____
_____
_____
_____
_____
_____
_____
_____

ACTIVITY

MEETING YOUR INNER SERVANT

Learning Goal

To gain wisdom and understanding about Service as the essence of a spirited team, through a dialogue with one's inner servant on being a servant in the organization.

Preparation

1. Photocopy the Reflection on Service, My Journey, and My Inner Servant handout for all participants.
2. Create a flip chart display with the heading, Service.

Learning Activity

1. Explain to participants that the thinking of Robert Greenleaf about Service was a major influence on *Building Team Spirit*. Robert Greenleaf's idea of the servant as leader came from reading Hermann Hesse's *Journey to the East*. Greenleaf writes in his groundbreaking book, *Servant Leadership*:

    In this story we see a band of men on a mythical journey, probably Hesse's own journey. The central figure of the story is Leo who accompanies the party as a servant who does their menial chores, but who also sustains them with his spirit and his song. He is a person of extraordinary presence. All goes well until Leo disappears. Then the group falls into disarray and the journey is abandoned. They cannot make it without the servant Leo. The narrator, one of the party, after some years of wandering finds Leo and is taken into the Order that had sponsored the journey. There he discovers that Leo, whom he had known first as servant, was in fact the titular head of the Order, its guiding spirit, a great and noble leader. (1977, p. 7)

2. Explain to participants that they will also be embarking on a journey to find and converse with their inner servants. At this time suggest that their inner servant may be some wise person they know—a grandfather or grandmother or other relative, a teacher, or perhaps some historical figure like St. Francis, Gandhi, Mother Theresa, Martin Luther King, or Eleanor Roosevelt.

3. Lead the participants through the following meditation:

> Allow your breathing to become slow and deep. [Pause for about 15 seconds.] Relax comfortably. Begin to release any tension in your body. [Pause for 15 seconds.]
>
> Bring to mind people who have been models of Service to you, such as good teachers, wise friends, or leaders. [Pause.] Consider the qualities that made them of Service to others and important models for you. [Pause for 20 to 30 seconds.]
>
> Now move more deeply into your appreciation of these figures and your willingness to be guided by their wisdom. [Pause.] You are about to take a journey where you will access your own deep wisdom.
>
> In a few moments, you will imagine yourself at the entrance of a large opening that provides access into the depths of the earth. It is the entrance into a magical world. Imagine the nature of this opening for yourself. It may be a hole in a large tree, a cliff overlooking the ocean, or a cave. [Pause.] With your next three breaths you will enter the opening. Feel yourself going deeper and deeper into this magical space.
>
> One. Two. Three. [Say very slowly.] Explore this enchanting place. [Pause for 20 to 30 seconds.]
>
> You are in a timeless and dreamlike reality. You feel your way and move bravely forward and downward on a path strangely familiar to you. Notice your sensations and feelings in this non-ordinary reality. Breathe deeply as you become more comfortable here. [Pause.]
>
> You move forward for a long while. You are starkly alone, lacking landmarks, acutely aware of your vulnerabilities and limited personal resources. Without knowing how, you have come to a monument, and on it are the beliefs and injunctions by which you have lived. Read one or more of them, and recognize that these have been your commandments. Take time to consider them. [Pause for 30 to 45 seconds.]
>
> You enter ever more deeply into the dark places of your being. You feel fully worthy of the guidance you desire regarding Service in your life. You anticipate meeting your Inner Servant, identified earlier. Moving beyond the monument, you eventually find yourself at a clearing surrounded by lush plants. At its edge, the branches of two large trees touch and form an archway. You know that on the other side of the archway is a strikingly beautiful place where you will find your Inner Servant. It may be a mountaintop, a desert, a cathedral, a body of water, a forest. Walk to the trees and notice how they form pillars for the archway that leads to your Inner Servant. Now step through the archway and behold this place. [Pause for 30 seconds.]

Respectfully walk up to and greet your Inner Servant. Notice the appearance of this extraordinary individual. [Pause.] Thank your Inner Servant for having met you. Use words, gestures, or silent intuitive communication. [Pause.] Recognize your Inner Servant's bottomless affection and belief in you. A profound silence falls upon you as you connect with your Inner Servant.

Ask your questions about what Service is ultimately about in your life. You may receive an unexpected answer. [Pause for 30 to 45 seconds.]

Now ask how you might come on a regular basis to visit. Your coming and going will be described to you in a way in which you learn best, perhaps by speaking, movement, or imagery. Remember that the laws of ordinary physics do not apply here. You may be told to find your way back by visualizing the paths you have already taken, by using the sound of a gong, a ritualized movement, or with the repetition of a few chosen words. Now with your Inner Servant's assurance that you can return, receive instruction on how to embark on your next visit. [Pause for 30 to 45 seconds.]

It is time to come back to ordinary reality. You will return in your own manner. Perhaps you will retrace your steps with the speed of a running deer, passing the monument, returning through the opening. Perhaps you will return in another way. Return now. [Pause for 20 seconds.]

Now you are back. You will, with your next three breaths, return to your ordinary reality. One. Two Three. [Say very slowly.] Coming into waking consciousness, gently open your eyes.

4. Provide all participants with the Reflection on Service, My Journey, and My Inner Servant handout. Have participants record their experience on the handout, emphasizing especially the method to be used for the next visit. Allow ten to fifteen minutes.

5. Ask participants to share any part of the experience that they feel comfortable about sharing with the group, drawing out ideas about Service as experienced by the participants. Record their ideas on the flip chart display.

What to Expect

This guided visualization moves participants to a different level of introspection and awareness. Occasionally, some participants report that their visualizations were superficial or unclear. Affirm all participants for what they saw or felt. There is no right or wrong interpretation; there is only what turned up for each individual participant. The written component at the end of the activity allows participants to make the awareness and images that they perceived in the visualization more concrete. The sharing about Service is typically at a thoughtful and enlightened level.

Approximate time: 60 minutes.

Reflections on what Service means to me, my journey, my inner servant, and the method I will use to return for my next visit.

_____
_____
_____
_____
_____
_____
_____
_____
_____
_____
_____
_____
_____
_____
_____
_____
_____
_____
_____
_____
_____
_____
_____
_____
_____
_____
_____
_____
_____
_____
_____

Photocopied from _Building Team Spirit_ by Barry Heermann.
Published by McGraw-Hill, ISBN 0-07-028472-5. To order, call 1-800-2MCGRAW.

REVEALING THE SPIRIT OF SERVICE—INDIVIDUAL

Learning Goal

To construct a succinct statement that reveals the essence of Service operating within individuals on the team.

Preparation

Photocopy the Spirit of Service handout for all participants.

Learning Activity

1. Suggest to team participants that there is a unique "spirit of Service" that operates at an inner level in all persons. This spirit of Service is the source of individual greatness. It is an incredibly powerful force. When named, acknowledged, and honored, it can transform one's relationship with life and work. This spirit of Service is unique to each individual. Most persons have not yet identified this inner gift.

2. Explain that the purpose of this activity is to support individual team members in identifying their spirit of Service. Naming an individual spirit of Service requires only a few words, choosing an "I" verb and a noun. While it is simply stated, it takes time to unearth and reveal the spirit of Service. In this activity we will begin the exploration that will help all team participants over time to name their spirit of Service.

3. Some illustrations of spirit of Service include:

   • initiating action;
   • insuring quality;
   • intuiting possibilities;
   • invoking the best in people;
   • instituting change;
   • impelling progress.

4. Distribute the Spirit of Service handout. Note that the handout provides two columns, one identifying "I" verbs and another for "spirit." In the space provided on the handout begin by recording qualities of spirit in the right hand column that your best friends, colleagues, and family or loved ones would share about you. Allow five minutes for thinking and writing. Then reflect on those aspirations that you most honor and cherish, and record them on the handout in the right-hand column. Scan the list and notice those words that pull or call you forth. Allow five minutes for this reflection and writing.

5. On the same handout, ask participants to review the list and identify "I" verbs that best communicate the spirit of Service for them. Note that they do not need to limit themselves to "I" verbs. Allow five minutes for this reflection and writing.

6. Clarify for participants that while it is useful to talk with colleagues and loved ones for feedback and perspective, they are the only ones who can ultimately unearth the essence operating deep within them. Suggest that they not rush their process, nor expect that they will arrive at their spirit of Service within the time limit of this activity. Request that they listen to their inner voices and intuition, and remind them that this process of listening may take days or weeks or longer to uncover the spirit that calls them forth. Reinforce the value of this investigation.

7. Ask that participants form triads for sharing their preliminary spirit of Service. Allow four minutes a person or twelve minutes for all three sharings. Request that participants use this time to pose questions and offer perspective that will guide their colleagues in discovering their spirit of Service.

8. Ask participants to share insights and awareness about exploring their spirit of Service.

9. At the next meeting of the team or during the next facilitation of a team spirit learning activity, ask team members to share their latest interpretations of their spirit of Service.

What to Expect

It is important to emphasize that everyone has a spirit of Service residing within, and that getting in touch with that spirit is an important endeavor. Be sure that participants understand that this activity is the starting point in this investigation, and that for some it requires considerable time to identify their spirit of Service. Impress upon participants that they will know when they have reached it because it will resonate powerfully with their own senses of identity.

Approximate time: 60 minutes.

1. In the space provided below, in the right-hand column, record words that describe qualities that your best friends, colleagues, and family or loved ones would share about you. Then reflect on those most honored and cherished aspirations and hopes that you feel operate within you. Scan the list and notice those words that "pull" or "call" you forth.
2. Then inspect the list of "I" verbs in the left-hand column and choose those that best communicate the spirit of service for you. The list of "I" verbs is not exhaustive. Feel free to use other verbs, not necessarily beginning with the letter "I," that are appropriate.

"I" verbs	Individual Spirit
igniting	_____
illuminating	_____
illustrating	_____
imagining	_____
imbuing	_____
impacting	_____
imparting	_____
impelling	_____
incurring	_____
inferring	_____
informing	_____
infusing	_____
initiating	_____
innovating	_____
instating	_____
instilling	_____
instituting	_____
institutionalizing	_____
insuring	_____
interposing	_____
interpreting	_____
introducing	_____
intuiting	_____
inventing	_____
inviting	_____
invoking	_____

Verbs

_____
_____
_____
_____
_____
_____
_____
_____
_____
_____
_____
_____
_____
_____
_____
_____
_____
_____
_____
_____
_____
_____
_____
_____
_____
_____
_____
_____
_____
_____
_____
_____
_____
_____

Individual Spirit

_____
_____
_____
_____
_____
_____
_____
_____
_____
_____
_____
_____
_____
_____
_____
_____
_____
_____
_____
_____
_____
_____
_____
_____
_____
_____
_____
_____
_____
_____
_____
_____
_____
_____

REVEALING THE SPIRIT OF SERVICE—TEAM

Learning Goals

1. To reveal the essence of Service operating within the team.
2. To construct a succinct statement of that essence of Service.

Preparation

1. Photocopy the Spirit of Team Service handout for all participants.
2. Create a flip chart display with the heading, Team Service: Working Title.

Learning Activity

1. Suggest to team participants that there is a unique "spirit of Service" that operates within the team. The spirit of Service is the source of team greatness. It is an incredibly potent and powerful force that when named, acknowledged, and honored can transform the team's relationship to those it serves.

2. Explain that the purpose of this activity is to enable the team to identify its spirit of Service. Naming the team's spirit of Service requires only the formation of a few words, choosing an "I" verb and a noun. While the result is simply stated, it takes time to unearth and reveal the spirit of Service. In this activity we will begin the exploration that leads to naming the team's spirit of Service.

3. Some illustrations of spirit of Service include:
   - insuring results;
   - invoking the future;
   - instilling pride;
   - institutionalizing quality;
   - initiating wonder;
   - infusing high performance.

263

4. Distribute the Spirit of Team Service handout. Note that the handout has two columns, one identifying "I" verbs and another headed "Spirit within the Team." Participants, working individually, begin by recording qualities of spirit in the right-hand column that they believe apply to the team when it is serving customers at its best. Allow five minutes for this reflection and writing. Instruct participants to scan the list and notice those words that best resonate with the spirit of this team. Allow five minutes for this reflection and writing.

5. On the same handout, ask participants to identify "I" verbs from the list that best communicate the team's spirit of Service. Suggest that this list of "I" verbs is not exhaustive, and that participants are free to use other verbs, not necessarily beginning with the letter "I," that they feel are appropriate. Allow five minutes for this reflection and writing.

6. Suggest that team participants not rush their process, nor expect that they will necessarily arrive at their team's spirit of Service within the time allowed for this activity. Request that they continue to investigate possibilities. It may require days, weeks, or longer to uncover the sprit that calls them forth. Reinforce the value of this investigation.

7. Based upon ideas generated from the handout, ask team participants to share their team's spirit of Service. Record all ideas on the flip chart display, and then facilitate a discussion with the team to begin to reach consensus about their spirit of Service. Allow 10 to 20 minutes for this brainstorming and discussion.

8. When the discussion is completed, request that team participants formulate a working title for their spirit of Service. Record their working title on the flip chart display. Allow ten minutes.

9. Ask team participants to share insights and awarenesses gained from exploring the team's spirit of Service.

10. When the team next meets for the facilitation of a team spirit learning activity, request that the team continue the dialogue and refine their spirit of Service statement.

What to Expect

This is a powerful activity for creating the purpose of the team in Service to customers and in Service of team members. Encourage the team to regularly remind each other of their spirit of Service. It should be incorporated into strategic documents and into mission, vision, and planning documents of the team. Discourage the team from forcing or focusing too quickly on a definition of their spirit of team Service.

Approximate time: 60-90 minutes.

Spirit of Team Service

1. In the space provided below, in the right-hand column, record words that describe qualities that best capture the team's spirit in delivering Service.
2. Then inspect the list of "I" verbs in the left-hand column and choose those that best communicate the team's spirit of service. The list of "I" verbs is not exhaustive. Feel free to use other verbs, not necessarily beginning with the letter "I," that are appropriate.

"I" verbs	Spirit within the Team
igniting	_____
illuminating	_____
illustrating	_____
imagining	_____
imbuing	_____
impacting	_____
imparting	_____
impelling	_____
incurring	_____
inferring	_____
informing	_____
infusing	_____
initiating	_____
innovating	_____
instating	_____
instilling	_____
instituting	_____
institutionalizing	_____
insuring	_____
interposing	_____
interpreting	_____
introducing	_____
intuiting	_____
inventing	_____
inviting	_____
invoking	_____

Verbs

Spirit within the Team

THE KEYS TO THE KINGDOM

Learning Goal

To create an understanding of the collective team notion of Service through exploration of the essence of Service and one additional phase of the Team Spirit Spiral that is pivotal to the team's effectiveness in providing Service.

Preparation

1. Photocopy the Archetypes for Phases of the Team Spirit Spiral handout for all participants.
2. Create three flip chart displays with the following headings:

   Service Archetype

   Archetypes and Their Functions

   Archetypes and Their Relationship to Enhancing Service

Note: Because this activity assumes understanding of the Team Spirit Spiral, use one of the following activities from Appendix D as a prelude to this activity: Walk in Nature: Discovering the Phases of the Spiral, or The Seasons of a Team's Life: Establishing Team Climate.

Learning Activity

1. Ask team participants to close their eyes and be restful. Allow several minutes of quiet, and then ask them, with their eyes closed and in a relaxed state, to imagine being in a favorite space. Ask that they create a mental image of that place and all the surrounding scenery, noticing the weather and their own internal state. Pause for 20 to 30 seconds. Have participants next imagine that a path appears before them and that they begin, with great pleasure, to traverse this path. Ask that they notice the

texture of the path and the surrounding vegetation and formations. Pause for 20 to 30 seconds, and then ask the team to imagine that a key appears on the ground before them on the pathway. Tell them to pick up the key and observe it. Ask:

   a. What does the key look like? [Suggest that they take time to savor the look and feel of the key.]
   b. What do you see as the function of the key?

Pause for 20 to 30 seconds.

2. Ask the group to slowly open their eyes and return as a full group. Explain that the key is symbolic, an archetype for Service. Ask participants to share with a colleague their images and intended uses of the key. Allow four minutes for each sharing, for a total of eight minutes, and then invite the full group to share their images of the key and what they have come to understand about Service and the role that it plays in the lives of individuals on the team and for the team in serving customers. Record all responses on the first flip chart display. Ask the team if there was any common pattern in the images for customer service. Ask for interpretations of how the respective individual notions of Service relate to the team's Service to its customers.

3. Upon completing this discussion explain to participants that you would like them to reflect on an additional archetypal form, this time for a phase of the Spiral that participants perceive as critical to heightened *team* effectiveness in serving each other. This may be a phase where the team experiences some dissonance.

4. Ask participants to consider and then select the phase of the Spiral that the team most needs to embrace and give active attention to. Allow two to three minutes for participants to reflect on and select that phase. Provide all participants with the Archetypes for Phases of the Team Spirit Spiral handout. Ask participants to notice the archetype associated with the phase that they selected. Allow one or two minutes for participants to reflect and to gain familiarity with the archetypal form associated with their phase.

5. Once again ask team participants to close their eyes and relax, keeping in mind their phase of the Spiral and the related archetype. Pause for 10 to 15 seconds, and then ask participants, with their eyes closed and in a relaxed state, to return to their favorite part of the world. Pause for 20 to 30 seconds, and then ask that they again create a mental image of that place in the world and the path that they were traversing, noticing

changes in their internal state. Pause briefly, and then ask them to begin again to traverse the path, and reflect on the phase of the Spiral that is important to enhancing their Service to customers. Ask them to recall the archetype, from the handout, that appears on or near the pathway. Pause for 20 to 30 seconds. Tell them to observe the archetype; pause briefly and then ask:

a. What does the [name the archetype] look like, observing all of the nuances of the archetype?

b. What do you see as the function of the archetype?

Pause for 20 to 30 seconds.

6. Ask the group to slowly open their eyes and to return as a full group. Ask participants to share their archetypes and their intended uses with a colleague. Allow four minutes for each sharing, for a total of eight minutes, and then invite the full group to share their respective images of archetypes and what they have come to understand about the role that they play in the life of the team.

7. Record archetypes and functions of archetypes on the second flip chart display. Allow 10 to 15 minutes for discussion.

8. Ask the team if there was any common pattern in the functions of archetypes. Ask for interpretations of how the respective individual functions of archetypes, and associated phases of the Spiral, relate to the team's work together in enhancing Service to customers or to the team. Record these ideas on the last flip chart display. Allow 10 to 15 minutes for discussion.

What to Expect

Participants have a good time and learn a great deal about themselves and about Service by interpreting the archetypes employed in this activity. The archetypes allow participants to come to a deeper understanding of Service and a phase of the Spiral that each person identified as important to the team. Exploration of archetypal forms leads toward developing concrete ways that the team can work together to enhance Service.

Approximate time: 60-90 minutes.

- Initiating: a door

- Visioning: eyeglasses

- Claiming: a ring [representing solidarity and commitment]

- Celebrating: a trophy [indicating award for accomplishment]

- Letting go: a gravestone [indicating the end of things]

FINDING THE GROUND THE TEAM STANDS ON

Learning Goals

1. To distinguish between outer (form and structure) and inner (spirit) dimensions of Service.

2. To integrate both dimensions into a coherent way of thinking that is shared by the team.

Preparation

1. Create a flip chart display with three headings at the top of the page: Flowers, Earth, and Roots.

2. Photocopy the Outer and Inner Dimensions of Service handout for all participants.

3. Create a flip chart display with two headings at the top of the page: Outer Dimensions of Service and Inner Dimensions of Service.

4. Create two flip chart displays with the headings: How We Would Look/How It Would Be Experienced and Action Steps.

Learning Activity

1. As a prelude to this activity on Service, ask the team to distinguish between the flowers of spring, the ground from which the flowers grow, and the roots of the flowers beneath the earth. Request that the team brainstorm these distinctions and record their responses on the first flip chart display, asking repeatedly, "What are the flowers symbolic of?" "What is the earth symbolic of?" and "What are the roots symbolic of?" (For example, for Flowers, new growth, blooming, outward formation, etc.; for Earth, nutrients, interface between new growth and roots, solidarity, etc.; for Roots, life source, origin of new growth, genesis, etc.) Allow ten minutes for this discussion.

2. Suggest to the team that it is useful to think of Service in metaphors. There are outer (form and structure) and inner (spirit) dimensions of Service. Distribute the Outer and Inner Dimensions of Service handout.

3. Engage participants in brainstorming characteristics of the unique outer and inner dimensions of Service for this team. For the outer — form and structure — dimension, assist the team by suggesting that these artifacts of the team include product and service characteristics and forms. For the inner — spirit — dimension, assist the team by suggesting that these are the deeper, unseen intentions, beliefs, values, and commitments the team holds about itself and customers. Brainstorm lists in both dimensions and record responses on the second flip chart display. Allow approximately 10 to 15 minutes for brainstorming.

4. Reinforce the point that most teams are focused on the outer dimension. Ask the team to consider what happens in teams and organizations when they are preoccupied with external forms. Allow five minutes for discussion.

5. Acknowledge that these outer dimensions are important, but emphasize that Service that is potentially transforming arises out of the inner dimension. Suggest that the two dimensions create an inseparable and unified whole. Ask the team to consider examples of organizations in which there is clearly a unification of the inner and outer dimensions (participants will sometimes suggest Apple Computers, the VW "bug" era of VW of America, etc.). Allow five minutes for discussion.

6. Based upon the earlier brainstorming in both dimensions, ask participants to image what this team would look like and how it would be felt and experienced by its members through a powerful synergy of inner and outer dimensions. Record these ideas on the third flip chart display. Allow five to ten minutes for discussion.

7. Ask the team to brainstorm action steps for realizing this synergy. Record these ideas on the last flip chart display. Allow five to ten minutes for discussion.

What to Expect

This is a powerful activity for creating awareness of the importance of spirit to great Service. The initial query into the symbolism of flowers, earth, and roots stretches the team to think metaphorically. Allow sufficient time for the team to reflect and generate ideas without rushing the instructions. Respect the silence in the room and allow the opportunity for the team to grapple with brainstorming outer and inner dimensions of spirit on this team. Encourage discussion related to how the team would experience a synergy of inner and outer dimensions.

Approximate time: 60 minutes.

Outer Dimension *Inner Dimension*

form and structure   *spirit*

products and
services

meaning, purpose,
and commitment to
customers and to team

Photocopied from *Building Team Spirit* by Barry Heermann.
Published by McGraw-Hill, ISBN 0-07-028472-5. To order, call 1-800-2MCGRAW.

Learning Goal

To enhance effectiveness in communicating with internal or external customers who have problem issues.

Preparation

1. Prepare a lecturette on the harmonics that operate within the Team Spirit Spiral (see Appendix C, lecturette 1), focusing the lecturette on dissonances that can occur in communications with clients.
2. Photocopy the Miracle Worker Planning Form handout for all participants.
3. Photocopy the Roles and Process Activity Form handout for all participants.
4. Photocopy the Miracle Worker Observation Form handout for all participants.

Learning Activity

1. Present a lecturette on the harmonics that operate within the Team Spirit Spiral, and clarify how dissonances can occur with clients and customers and how an effective method of communication can turn dissonances into consonances. Engage the group in a discussion of the value of providing straight, clear, communication to customers and working together toward a solution that can lead to enhanced customer service and consonant relationship.
2. Request that each participant think of a client or customer with whom he or she is currently experiencing difficulty or with whom there is some opportunity for enhancing the relationship. Explain that participants will have an opportunity to respond to this customer during this learning

activity and to take advantage of the coaching that is available from team members. Allow two to three minutes.

3. Stress that the art of communicating with customers draws upon subtle speaking and listening skills. It requires listening, at a deep level, to customer concerns and needs, so that they know they are being heard fully and completely. It requires speaking in such a way that customers feel their needs and concerns are being responded to and that they understand our commitment to serving them. Generate ideas from participants about the necessary characteristics of effective communications with their customers. Record these on the flip chart display.

4. If cofacilitating this module, you may want to model effective speaking and listening skills with your partner, who would take on the role of a hypothetical customer. Allow ten minutes.

5. Explain that the team will now enter into a rehearsal for supporting a client with a problem issue. Distribute the Roles and Process for the Miracle Worker Activity Form. Clarify the three key roles: the communicator (the person who will deliver the communication), the receiver (the person who will play the customer), and the observer (a colleague from the team who will take notes and facilitate a feedback session at the completion of the practice). All participants will have a chance to serve in each of the three roles.

6. Ask the team members to recall and clarify in their minds the relationship they have with a particular client who has a current issue to resolve. Suggest that they choose a customer who is key to producing some important team result. Distribute the Miracle Worker Planning Form, and explain the use of the handout. Ask team members to take the time to write the answers to the questions before beginning the process.

7. After completing the questions, ask selected team members to share their insights. Ask team members to share their intentions for communicating with their customers as well as pitfalls that might decrease their effectiveness. Allow ten minutes.

8. Return participants to the Roles and Process Activity Form, clarifying the three phases of the rehearsal. Within two minutes the communicator gives the receiver details about the individual to whom he or she intends to communicate and how that person is likely to respond. The second phase provides for the actual communication (eight minutes). The third phase allows for the communicator to reflect on what worked and didn't work about the way the communication was delivered. This is followed by the receiver (customer) providing feedback on what worked and didn't

work, followed by the observer who provides a synthesis, referring to the notes taken on an observation sheet about the communicator's effectiveness. Caution: During the feedback phase the observer will be tempted to respond first. Emphasize that the observers should resist this temptation, allowing the communicator and the receiver the first chance to reflect and respond. Distribute the Miracle Worker Observation Form, and clarify the use of this form. Ask if there are any questions.

9. Explain that the rehearsal will last 45 minutes, 15 minutes per round, and that you will be warning the team when there are a few minutes left in each 15-minute round. Reinforce the time lines described earlier and stress that the observer should monitor the time. Clarify that each person will have a chance to serve in each of the three roles and that you will be circulating among the rehearsal groups.

10. Determine if there are any questions. Instruct team members to have their answers to the planning questions and the observation form in front of them. Remind observers to write legibly so they can give their written comments to the communicator at the end of the round. Clarify that you will be announcing when they should advance from round to round.

11. When there are no further questions, count off by threes. Ask each triad to go to an area of the room where they will not be disturbed by others and to choose who will start as the communicator, the receiver, and the observer for the first round. Let the group know that you or your cofacilitator may join a triad, providing your observations and feedback during the feedback phase.

12. Instruct the triads to begin the first round. Carefully monitor the time, letting each group know when there are a few minutes remaining so they can complete their feedback. Circulate among the triads through the three rounds.

13. When all three rounds are completed, debrief the full team. Ask, What did you learn that will contribute to your being effective in communicating with customers? What worked? What didn't work?

What to Expect

This exercise provides valuable skill development for communicating with customers about sensitive issues. A didactic component engages participants in discussion of the challenge of facing the difficult customer. Skills are practiced in the rehearsal. Participants will gain most by focusing on their experience in a current customer relationship.

This module will deepen awareness about the challenges and opportunities of communicating with customers about difficult situations. The key to effective facilitation of the skill component is crisp, clear instructions on the rehearsal, including:

- the three rehearsal roles,
- the requirements of each rehearsal phase,
- the timing of each rehearsal phase, and
- the handouts used in conjunction with the rehearsal.

It is useful to repeat instructions for the rehearsal, asking if participants have questions. The discussion following the skill component provides the opportunity for team members to share their experiences and to grasp the importance of good communications with customers.

Approximate time: 60-90 minutes.

Miracle Worker Planning Form

1. What is your goal in communicating with this customer?

_____

_____

_____

_____

_____

_____

2. What are the relevant facts, issues, and situations from the customer's perspective?

_____

_____

_____

_____

_____

_____

3. What suggestions/ideas/possibilities might you offer to the customer?

_____

_____

_____

_____

_____

_____

4. What do you need to be mindful of about yourself in order to make a difference with this customer regarding his or her needs and concerns?

_____

_____

_____

_____

_____

_____

Photocopied from *Building Team Spirit* by Barry Heermann.
Published by McGraw-Hill, ISBN 0-07-028472-5. To order, call 1-800-2MCGRAW.

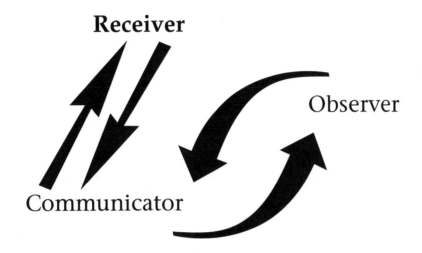

	Phase 1 Preparation 2 minutes	Phase 2 Communication 8 minutes	Phase 3 Feedback 5 minutes
Communicator			
Receiver			
Observer			

1. Did the communicator effectively communicate his or her goal to the customer?

_____

_____

_____

_____

_____

2. Did the communicator effectively communicate the relevant facts, issues, and situations from the customer's perspective?

_____

_____

_____

_____

_____

3. Did the communicator effectively communicate suggestions/ideas/possibilities that responded to the customer's needs?

_____

_____

_____

_____

_____

4. Did the communicator effectively communicate and make a difference with this customer regarding the customer's needs and concerns?

_____

_____

_____

_____

_____

Photocopied from *Building Team Spirit* by Barry Heermann.
Published by McGraw-Hill, ISBN 0-07-028472-5. To order, call 1-800-2MCGRAW.

Learning Goals

1. To develop awareness of the power of archetypes as a way to reveal the team's spirit of Service.
2. To choose archetypes that best "fit" the team's spirit of Service.

Preparation

1. Photocopy the Common Archetypal Symbols handout for all participants.
2. Photocopy the Team Archetypal Symbols handout for all participants.
3. Create two flip chart displays with the headings, Sample Symbols and Team Symbols.

Learning Activity

Background: Renowned Swiss psychologist Carl Jung identified archetypes as the deep structures that mirror our feelings, hopes, fears, and spirit. Archetypes emerge from what Jung called the "collective unconscious." The unconscious, according to Jung, contains multiple levels of knowledge and experience from the combined history of all humanity. Jung's claim to this theory was based upon consistent repetitive reporting by his patients of common archetypal symbols. *Note:* For the purpose of this activity the word symbol substitutes for the word archetype because of its broad accessibility, though archetype more accurately reflects the Jungian concept. Whether to use the word archetype is left to the discretion of the facilitator.

1. Explain that symbols are powerful images that provide understanding and insight about substance and direction in life. These symbols exist at the level of the individual and at the level of team and organization. Individuals, teams, and organizations in industrialized nations are

increasingly isolated from the subtle messages conveyed through nature and intuitive knowing. The intensity and pace of modern organizations drown out the subtle messages that serve as guideposts for individuals and organizations. Symbols are a way to reveal the team's spirit.

2. In this activity we will explore the deeper implications of the spirit to the team. Emphasize that this is important work to do as symbols capture the critical linkage or bridge between the realm of spirit and the realm of form and structure. Symbols lead the team to examine their beliefs. They are powerful. They express the way the team thinks, feels, and behaves. These images literally create the circumstances of the team's life and define the possibility for extraordinary Service.

3. Distribute the Common Archetypal Symbols handout. Ask the participants to scan the list of symbols in each of the various categories identified on the handout. Request that team members take their time, reflecting on each one, circling up to six or creating their own symbols (in the space provided at the end of the Common Archetypal Symbols handout) that best capture the spirit of this team. Allow 10 to 15 minutes for participants to choose symbols.

4. Ask one participant to share one of his or her choices, and engage the team in an exploration of the deep meaning associated with this image (e.g., cave might engender responses such as darkness, adventure, womb, and birth; or bear might generate responses such as strength, power, hibernation, and introspection). Record the responses on the first flip chart display. Now ask team members to identify the meanings associated with each of the half-dozen symbols they identified, recording their thoughts on the Team Symbols handout. Ask participants to use stream of consciousness writing, letting go of grammar, punctuation, and other writing restrictions, with the intention of getting to the critical qualities of spirit that are at the core of the Service the team provides. Allow 10 to 15 minutes for this discussion and writing.

5. When they have finished writing about their symbols, request that participants choose one or two that best capture the spirit of the team, sharing their choices with their colleagues. Record these symbols on the second flip chart display. Ask the team to consider common patterns across symbols. Work with the team to reach consensus on a common symbol or combination of several symbols that best typifies this team.

6. (Optional.) Determine beforehand if there is anyone on the team who is artistically talented and is willing to create a rendering of the agreed-upon archetypal symbol. If there is no one who is artistically gifted on the team, determine if there is a team colleague who is able to create a

computer graphic of the symbol. If these kinds of skills are not present on the team, suggest that the team contract a graphic artist to create such a rendering for the team.

What to Expect

Participants find access to new ways of thinking and sharing about the spirit of Service operating within the team. A key to successfully facilitating this activity is to allow full expression of all team member symbols, reaching consensus among the team about the main symbol or combination of symbols.

Approximate time: 60-75 minutes.

Natural Phenomena

thunder	tidal wave	tide	volcano	waterfall
weather	wave	wind	planets	quicksand
rain	rainbow	sky	snow	lightning
mist	night	ocean	chaos	clouds
dawn	earth	electricity	earthquake	fire
forest	glacier	jungle	lake	valley
light	meadow	mountain	oasis	rust
storm	summer	spring	beach	cave
cliff	diamond	hills	ice	island
pond	path	smoke	pit	flame
heat	hole	knock		

Human Physiology

teeth	throat	thumb	womb	mouth
cancer	pain	perspiration	pregnancy	sex
hair	stomach	arms	birth	blood
deaf	head	hand	death	ears
eyes	face	heart	illness	nakedness
little finger	lungs	miscarriage	nose	

Artifacts from Nature

trees	water	web	well	willow
wings	acorn	ashes	cobwebs	cocoon
flowers	leaves	lily	lotus	mud
nest	oak	oil	pearl	quartz
rock	rose	sand	seeds	shell
stones	feather	sunflower	magnet	cactus
gold	icicles	metal	river	

Photocopied from *Building Team Spirit* by Barry Heermann.
Published by McGraw-Hill, ISBN 0-07-028472-5. To order, call 1-800-2MCGRAW.

Foods

apple	grain	lemon	nut	oil
olive	onion	orange	peach	pepper
prune	salt	egg	tea	popcorn
milk	meat	food		

Living Creatures

tiger	turtle	vulture	wasp	whale
wolf	worm	leopard	lion	lizard
monkey	moth	mouse	mule	ostrich
owl	parrot	peacock	pig	porcupine
ram	rat	salmon	sheep	shark
skunk	snail	snake	spider	sponge
squirrel	swan	bat	bear	bee
bird	butterfly	cat	caterpillar	crow
fish	frog	goose	hawk	horse
kangaroo	ladybug	deer	dog	dolphin
rabbit				

Human Made Artifacts

table	tape	telephone	telescope	temple
tent	thread	tightrope	tires	toilet
tomb	tower	toys	train	treadmill
tunnel	umbrella	velvet	wall	wand
watch	weaving	wine	yo-yo	altar
anchor	arrow	balloon	bank	bed
boat	books	bridge	bowl	cage
candle	cemetery	chain	chalice	church
clock	coffin	compass	convent	cross
dam	door	drum	dynamite	fence
floor	fountain	garden	gate	glass
glasses	glove	glue	grave	gun
home/house	hospital	jail	jewel	key
keyhole	menorah	pie	piano	pill
pillar	porch	pot	pottery	prayer beads
puppet	purse	puzzle	pyramid	quilt
radio	rags	refrigerator	ring	revolving door
road	robot	roof	room	rope
sail	saddle	sailboat	saw	scissors

Human Made Artifacts (Continued)

seesaw	shield	shoes	signs	soap
stage	stairs	steel	letter	library
lock	luggage	machine	mail	mandala
map	mask	message	medicine	merry-go-round
microscope	mirror	money	museum	music
nail	oar	observatory	orchard	oven
parachute	pen	pencil	penny	pendulum
perfume	photograph	pocket	net	laser
package	luggage	sword	saw	radar
musical instrument				

Musical Images

jazz ensemble	orchestra	symphony	tempo	credenza
dissonance	consonance	chord	discord	harmony
melody	crescendo			

Human Relationships/Roles

teacher	uncle	aunt	virgin	waiter/waitress
male	man	mother	father	nun
nurse	orphan	parents	pioneer	pirate
police	prince	princess	prisoner	prostitute
Quaker	queen	robber	shepherd	slave
soldier	child	Christ	clown	doctor
female	god	goddess	grandfather	grandmother
guru	king	saint		

Fantasy Images

treasure	unicorn	vampire	witch	angel
demon	devil	dragon	fairy	heaven
hell	shadow	stork	magician	maze
monster	paradise			

Shapes/Images

triangle	abyss	circle	colors	crack
emptiness	square	open	swastika	spiral

Planetary/Geographic Landmarks

sun	moon	Mars	stars	Mercury
north	south	east	west	Venus

Human Capacity/Demonstrative Act

war	love	wedding	whistle	play
quest	rage	rescue	sacrifice	suicide
magic	marriage	martyr	meditation	mourning
nightmare	fear	fight	heal/healer	kiss
crying	laughing	sleeping	vacation	holy

Activities

party	poker	rowing	running	swimming
parade	sailing			

Other symbols that represent my team's spirit:

_____

_____

_____

_____

_____

_____

_____

_____

_____

Photocopied from *Building Team Spirit* by Barry Heermann.
Published by McGraw-Hill, ISBN 0-07-028472-5. To order, call 1-800-2MCGRAW.

Team Archetypal Symbols

Archetype #1

_____
_____
_____

Archetype #2

_____
_____
_____

Archetype #3

_____
_____
_____

Archetype #4

_____
_____
_____

Archetype #5

_____
_____

Archetype #6

_____
_____
_____

Photocopied from *Building Team Spirit* by Barry Heermann.
Published by McGraw-Hill, ISBN 0-07-028472-5. To order, call 1-800-2MCGRAW.

Part III

APPENDICES

A

Guidelines for Using the Team Spirit Assessment and Facilitating the Feedback and Action Planning Session

The Team Spirit Assessment can be successfully used as a learning activity as described in Appendix D or it may be used in a more in-depth way as part of an all-day Feedback and Action Planning Session. The following guidelines provide for an in-depth use of the Team Spirit Assessment.

THE FEEDBACK AND ACTION PLANNING SESSION

In the Feedback and Action Planning Session it is important to set the context for the use of the Team Spirit Assessment.

Clarify for the team that in order to change its relationship from one of dissonance to one of greater consonance there are three critical considerations that need to be in place.

Facilitate a discussion of the importance of all three components.

- *Data on the harmonics operating within the team (which the Team Spirit Assessment provides).*

- *A shared approach and team development model (which Team Spirit provides).*

- *A commitment to improve team effectiveness (which only the team can provide).*

The following graphic suggests the major components of the Feedback and Action Planning Session:

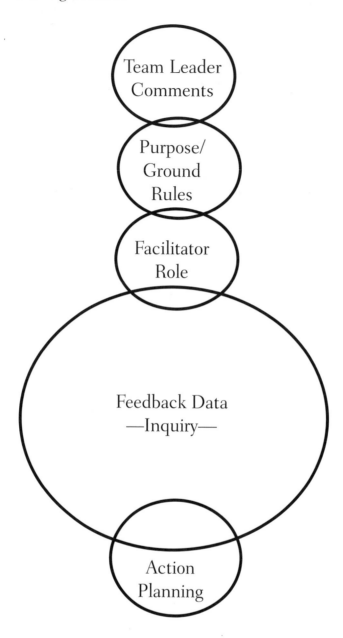

The organization of the agenda for the Feedback and Action Planning Session is as follows:

- Introduction/Goals/Ground Rules

- Presentation of the Team Spirit Assessment data (goal: team takes ownership of data)

- Discussion of key issues (What are the gaps between the data and the team's expectations?)

- Design of specific actions that respond to dissonances

- Completion

The following guidelines suggest the parameters of the Feedback and Action Planning Session.

1. Introduce the team leader who will provide introductions and expectations of the Feedback and Action Planning Session.

   Coach the team leader on how to create a climate for an effective feedback session—expressing commitment to the process and encouraging openness and authenticity.

2. Present the agenda for the Feedback and Action Planning Session. Create with the team the ground rules and purpose for the session, posting both on a flip chart.

   The Facilitator should restate his or her role: "My role is to reflect back to you what the data reveal about your work together as a team and to support you in deciding what to do about it." Clarify that they will probably not resolve all of the issues today, but that they will take a significant stride. Ask participants if they agree to operate under the ground rules and achieve the purpose of the feedback session.

3. Administer the Team Spirit Assessment (see page 309).

   a. Provide copies of the Team Spirit Assessment to all team members.

   b. Stress that participants should be honest when placing their checkmarks on the harmonics continuums on the Team Spirit Assessment, identifying the point on the ten-point scale that best reflects, from their individual perspective, where the team is functioning in relationship with the dissonant and consonant items.

   c. When all participants have completed their Assessments, request that they convert their checkmarks to a number score, recording it on the right side of the page in the margin. Note that a consonant factor is rated 10 and a dissonant factor 1.

4. Review the Team Spirit Assessment mean scores posted on a flip chart in a prominent part of the room. With the team, identify and list all consonances, acknowledging the team for its excellence. List and prioritize all issues (dissonances) resulting from a discussion of the data presented in the Team Spirit Assessment.

Review the Assessment item by item, and ask participants to generate concrete examples of both consonances and dissonances. Confront participants when they drift into abstraction or gloss over difficult issues, returning them to concrete examples. Urge team members to be forthright and "own" their data.

List key issues on a flip chart as participants identify them. Ask participants to find overlapping issues and concerns. Invite them to prioritize critical concerns and issues.

5. Facilitate the development of action plans that respond to the issues.

Focus on one to two of the key issues. Emphasize the need to create concrete changes in behavior in the team. As a part of the action planning phase, pose the following kinds of questions:

- What do you need to do right now to move ahead regarding "x"?
- What are the key obstacles that might get in the way?
- How will you prevent these obstacles from getting in the way?
- What specifically are you going to do in the next week? The next month?

6. Acknowledge the participation of team members. Facilitate completion and acknowledge and provide feedback to participants.

In conclusion, after an effective Feedback and Action Planning Session the team should leave the session feeling that they have been heard and understood and that they have planned a series of agreed-upon actions that respond to their needs.

```
┌─────────────────────────────────────────────────────────┐
│                                                           │
│              Team Spirit Assessment                       │
│                                                           │
└─────────────────────────────────────────────────────────┘
```

1. Service

contribution |—|—|—|—|—|—|—|—| depletion

aligned execution |—|—|—|—|—|—|—|—| uncoordinated action

mutual support |—|—|—|—|—|—|—|—| unsupportiveness

2. Initiating

orientation |—|—|—|—|—|—|—|—| disorientation

belonging |—|—|—|—|—|—|—|—| alienation

trust |—|—|—|—|—|—|—|—| mistrust

3. Visioning

shared vision/values |—|—|—|—|—|—|—|—| ambiguous vision/values

compassion |—|—|—|—|—|—|—|—| callousness

presence |—|—|—|—|—|—|—|—| aridness

4. Claiming

goal/role alignment |—|—|—|—|—|—|—|—| nonalignment

organization support |—|—|—|—|—|—|—|—| nonsupport

competence |—|—|—|—|—|—|—|—| deficiency

5. Celebrating

appreciation |—|—|—|—|—|—|—|—| nonappreciation

energy |—|—|—|—|—|—|—|—| burnout

wonder |—|—|—|—|—|—|—|—| disenchantment

6. Letting Go

disclosure |—|—|—|—|—|—|—|—| withheld communication

constructive |—|—|—|—|—|—|—|—| criticism

feedback completion |—|—|—|—|—|—|—|—| incompletion

B

Guidelines for Conducting Effective Team Interviews

HOW TO CONDUCT AN OPEN-ENDED, QUALITATIVE DIAGNOSIS (I.E., PERSONAL INTERVIEWS) TO DETERMINE THE NEEDS OF THE TEAM

When working with mature teams it is critical that diagnostic work be conducted to determine the most appropriate combination of learning activities to support team needs. Such diagnostic work ideally consists of qualitative interviews as the most effective means to gain understanding of the team.

The benefits of personal interviews:

1. They use open-ended questioning, allowing the facilitator to uncover subtle implications of the team's dynamics in each of the phases of the Team Spirit Spiral.

2. They deepen the facilitator's understanding of underlying issues and possibilities related to the team's developmental needs.

3. They provide useful subjective feedback—key impressions, awareness, insights.

4. They allow for additional probing into critical factors related to the unique harmonics, that is, the pattern of consonance and dissonance, operating in the team.

Such qualitative diagnostic work inquires into all of the phases of the Team Spirit Spiral, from Initiating, Visioning, Claiming, Celebrating, and Letting Go to Service.

Schedule interviews with a representative cross section of the team for approximately 30 minutes each. Take careful notes throughout the interviews. These interview notes become a part of the confidential file that is maintained for that team. Allow 15 minutes between interviews to organize notes before beginning the next interview.

The purpose of the qualitative interview is to gather important subjective data, impressions, or ideas that will lead to recommendations to the team about the composition of guided experiences that will best advance team spirit and effectiveness. A schedule of questions that you may draw upon for the diagnostic interviews is presented below.

At the interviews, introduce yourself and assure the team member that you will be treating his or her responses confidentially. Begin with open-ended questions. For example, "I'd appreciate your sharing your experience of serving on this team. What is working in this team? What isn't working in this team? What is the one improvement in the team that you would like to see occur that would best advance the team's spirit and effectiveness? What are the team's major strengths and counterproductive tendencies?"

Based upon the responses to these open-ended questions you may choose to probe more deeply into the phases of the Team Spirit Spiral. Consider extending your inquiry with some combination of the following questions.

Initiating

1. Does your team take time to welcome new members and make them feel comfortable?
2. Describe the state of trust among team members.

Visioning

1. Describe the level of excitement your team feels about its intended mission and purpose.
2. Describe your team's vision and values. How did your team formulate vision and values?

Claiming

1. Are team members, clear about their goals and roles?
2. How does your team achieve the necessary skills and resources to accomplish its goals?

Celebrating

1. How does your team experience appreciation for the work that they produce?
2. Does your team celebrate its victories?

Letting Go

1. Describe the degree of honesty and clarity your team achieves in its communications.
2. How do team members provide constructive feedback to each other?

Service

1. Describe your team's commitment to serving customers.
2. Provide examples of ways that team members serve and honor customers (internal and external).

C

Lecturettes

LECTURETTE 1: TEAM SPIRIT SPIRAL AND HARMONICS

Key point number 1: The "spirit" in Team Spirit

Just as scientists have revealed atomic particles as the unseen but essential building blocks of the physical universe, the defining characteristic of the high-performing team is this unseen but critical "spirit." The elusive quality of spirit will be experienced through team spirit learning activities.

Spirit is not separate from worldly affairs, nor is spirit some ephemeral or ambiguous state. It is at the core of our humanity, including our work together in groups and teams, should we choose to notice and cultivate it. Team spirit is a process for becoming more conscious of spirit in work and for fostering spirited teams.

Spirit is the committed exploration for meaning and purpose in life and work. It inspires us. It draws us beyond ourselves. In moving beyond narrow self-interest, beyond the individualism that permeates our culture, the possibility of extraordinary teams emerges. Spirit is at the core of this possibility, and team spirit is the desired end state.

Key point number 2: The qualities of spirit present in high-performing teams

While at some level spirit defies cognitive understanding, we can name qualities of spirit operating in teams. Identifying these qualities provides a common vocabulary for teams to reflect on their work together. Here are the six qualities represented as "phases" of a spiral (refer to a pre-prepared flip chart display of the Team Spirit Spiral with each phase written in a different color):

1. **The Core integrating phase of Service**
   Quality of spirit: The experience of contribution and service to customers and to the team.

2. **The Initiating phase**
   Quality of spirit: A profound sense of relationship, wherein team members feel belonging and trust in their work together.

3. **The Visioning phase**
   Quality of spirit: An extraordinary sense of possibility for what can be created, that is alive and present for the team.

4. **The Claiming phase**
   Quality of spirit: The experience of team solidarity, single-minded purpose, and assurance about what needs to be accomplished.

5. **The Celebrating phase**
   Quality of spirit: The presence of awe, wonder, and an appreciation for the contribution of the team and team members.

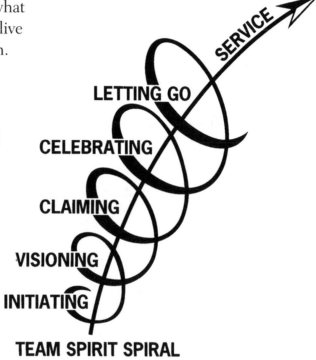

6. **The Letting Go phase**
   Quality of spirit: A sense of freedom and completion that arises from being forthright and sharing with full integrity.

The qualities of spirit represented in the Spiral interact in complex ways, as they blend and fuse throughout the life of the team. For example, the quality of spirit, Letting Go, is ideally occurring in every phase of the team's work together.

Key point number 3: Overview of the harmonics within each phase of the Spiral

Using music as a metaphor for building team spirit provides a way to understand group values and dynamics. All teams have distinct harmonic patterns. Accordingly, the underlying values structure integral to team spirit is expressed in terms of harmonics.

Each phase of the Team Spirit Spiral has its own unique harmonics, combining both consonant factors and dissonant factors. Just as in great music, teams are animated and enlivened by drawing on *both* consonances and dissonances.

Most teams welcome the consonant and avoid the dissonant. In music, dissonance leads to resolution. In teams, embracing the dissonance moves the team to a position of strength, ultimately leading to a more spirited team and to heightened Service.

Note: The following portion of this lecturette provides a fuller presentation of the harmonics operating within each phase.

Consider the interplay of harmonics at each phase of the Team Spirit Spiral. The existence of dissonance in a phase or phases is an indication to the team that it needs to place emphasis on that phase or phases.

SERVICE

At the core of the Team Spiral is Service. Delighting customers and contributing to others is essential to high-performing teams. Extraordinary Service arises out of the work the team has done in the Initiating, Visioning, and Claiming phases of the Spiral. Service includes the provision of products or services to enrich the worlds of other individuals or organizations. Consonant factors associated with Service include: committed action that leads to significant contribution to customers, and joy, passion, and delight in ministering to those served by the team. Successful Service reflects a splendid realization of vision, and the experience of mutual support and contribution by team members and customers.

Dissonant signs that prompt greater attention to responding to the team include: feelings of lack of support, depletion of energy among team members, or uncoordinated action in the delivery of Service.

INITIATING

Individuals called together in teams often feel a discontinuity during team formation. This dissonant quality is to be expected. It is healthy. It can sensitize team members to individual needs and the needs of the team as a whole. These needs include understanding the purpose of the team and the contribution each team member might make to the realization of that purpose.

When a team successfully engages in Initiating work, members of the team achieve the consonant qualities of belonging, positive orientation, and mutual trust. This self-understanding permeates the team, empowering it to define and accomplish its work effectively.

Signs of dissonance in the form of mistrust, fear, or disorientation among team members signal a need for the team to place greater focus on Initiating.

VISIONING

Visioning and Initiating are highly interdependent phases of the Spiral, and for some teams Visioning may precede the work of Initiating. The solid base of relationship that Initiating provides allows a powerful basis for Visioning, and the reverse is also true. Visioning engages the team in consideration of the very essence of its work. The team distinguishes current reality from the ideal reality (i.e., vision) it holds for the future. Out of Visioning comes consonance as the team clarifies its purpose, core values and beliefs, and a most extraordinary future sense of how customers might be served. As a result of successful Visioning the team is enlivened and is "present" to the possibility of their work together.

When vision and values are unclear, dissonance occurs within teams. Such dissonant factors as callousness regarding those the team serves and ambiguous vision or values suggests the need to revisit the Visioning phase.

The dissonant experience of emptiness or aridness within the team conveys that the team is not "present" to its possibility to serve generously.

CLAIMING

The development of relationship and awareness of team vision experienced in the first two phases of the Spiral lead to Claiming. Claiming involves the team in taking ownership of goals and roles for its work together, based upon shared vision and values.

Consonant factors associated with Claiming include: alignment of team members with the goals of the team, commitment to the growth and development of team members, ownership of team roles, and the team's capacity to secure needed organizational support.

When the team's work in Claiming is dissonant, typical signs include invalidation of the team or the work it undertakes, feelings of inadequacy, and lack of agreement regarding goals or roles.

CELEBRATING

Successful Service engenders Celebrating. The spirit of the team is ignited and nurtured in Celebrating. This phase of the Spiral is life-giving and nurtures the further work of the team. It provides a sense of unity and spirit.

Consonant factors operating within Celebrating include feelings of being appreciated and acknowledged within the team, a sense of unbounded energy and the capacity to "move mountains." Celebrating is characterized by a sense of wonder that pervades the team generating a desire to "do it again."

When team members feel unappreciated, disenchanted, or burned out, it is important that teams recognize the resulting "dis-ease" and respond to the dissonance, creating the missing sense of appreciation and spirit within the team. Such transformations may arise through work in the final phase of the Spiral, Letting Go.

LETTING GO

The consonant factors characteristic of successful Letting Go are forthrightness, disclosure, and constructive feedback, freely given and received. These characteristics are not only acceptable in the team, but safely practiced and welcomed.

When the team experiences dissonance in the form of withheld communication or tension and disintegration in relationships, it is a signal to the team to find ways to begin Letting Go. Letting Go allows for new beginnings, for initiation, for a future not based in the past.

Breakdowns occur in the best teams. An array of dissonances can develop within the team. Team members experience disappointment when the intended service is *not* provided. Team members can become frustrated with the performance of other team members or others in the organization. Conflict can even occur as a result of committed team members having honest differences of opinion about how best to serve the customer. In short, even in quite successful teams there is a dark side. Although our experience of it may be agitation, anxiety, sadness, or anger, this dark side offers creative opportunities.

If we value embracing and confronting the problems in a constructive way, rather than withholding feelings or repressing differences, Letting Go can be powerfully transforming. The key is to provide the space, time, safety, and opportunity for "truth-telling" within the team.

Significant forces work against spirit in teams. Years of conditioning elevate and enshrine individualism. Organizations exalt form and structure, relegating the unseen, the spirit of the team, to unconsciousness. Organizations ignore or respond ineptly to the needs of the spirit. Intolerant of problems and ambiguity, organizations rely on aggressive individuals or on form and structure to find their healing and purpose. It isn't there.

Embracing team spirit, in all of its various manifestations—both its light and shadow sides, is critical to significant team and organization renewal.

LECTURETTE 2: IMPLICATIONS OF THE TEAM SPIRIT SPIRAL FOR INDIVIDUALS

Key point number 1: The Team Spirit Spiral speaks to individuals as well as teams

The Team Spirit Spiral provides guidance for developing inspired, high-performing individuals, as well as teams and organizations. The phases of the Team Spirit Spiral identify the paths that individuals can take to enhance consonances and identify and work through personal dissonances.

Review the Operational Levels of Team Spirit handout (see the Team Member Handout in the Personal Spiral activity in Chapter 3). The Spiral is a useful way to consider the dynamics of whole organizations, interpersonal relationships, and personal development as well as team development. Notice particularly the intrapersonal consideration on the handout. Individuals experience the phases of the Spiral in their own lives, in their relationships with their family and friends, at work, and in all aspects of their day-to-day affairs. For most persons there exists a pattern in how we relate to the Spiral phases that cuts across all dimension of living, whether family or work related.

Key point number 2: The phases of the Spiral related to individual development

Our unique pattern of consonances and dissonances tend to be present in both our personal and our work lives. Consider each of the phases of the Spiral and their implications at a personal level in all aspects of life:

Service: the experience of contribution to others.

Initiating: a profound sense of relationship, wherein one feels belonging and trust.

Visioning: an extraordinary sense of possibility for what can be created, that is alive and present.

Claiming: the experience of single-minded purpose and assurance about what needs to be accomplished.

Celebrating: the presence of awe, wonder, and an appreciation for others.

Letting Go: a sense of freedom and completion that arises from being forthright and sharing with full integrity.

Facilitating Awareness about the Team Spirit Spiral

We join spokes together in a wheel,
but it is the center hole that makes the wagon move.
We shape clay into a pot, but it is the emptiness
inside that holds whatever we want.
We hammer wood for a house,
but it is the inner space that makes it livable.
Tao Te Ching, translation by Stephen Mitchell

Objective scientific thinking is a paradox for modern enterprises. On one level it has served us well. Scientific management has contributed to our understanding of organization and team effectiveness. However, scientific management is only part of the story. Science asserts and modern enterprise generally accepts: "If you can't see it, it's not real," "You can only trust data received through your five senses," and "What can't be measured can't be." This kind of thinking has obscured spirit.

When spirit is neglected, organizations become sterile and empty places. Such environments diminish the physical and emotional well-being of workers. Workers may respond to the lifelessness of their workplaces with obsessive, compulsive, and addictive behaviors. Organizational effectiveness diminishes. The decline in effectiveness, the uncertainty, the emptiness, and the crises that are experienced push individuals and organizations to deeper investigation into what is critical in life and work.

Building Team Spirit is designed to help facilitators respond to this crisis of "spirit." By paying attention to matters of spirit at work we can transform our relationships with associates and with those we serve, thus fostering high-performing, spirited teams and organizations.

When we nourish the spirit, we experience connectedness, balance, and a sense of freedom. Attending to the spirit creates space for extraordinary possibilities, harmony, and achievement beyond our wildest dreams. It is at the heart of high performance.

Spirit is not some remote concept separate from mainstream living. Spirit is present in all of life. When we allow ourselves to become consciously aware of spirit something extraordinary happens. Everyday work is filled with possibility and excitement.

This appendix of learning activities creates the context for spirit in teams, fosters emotional and spiritual ownership, and provides cognitive understanding of team spirit and its values. These activities serve an additional purpose. They provide the facilitator with exposure to the team to determine its unique needs and dynamics. This knowledge allows the facilitator to choose the learning activities that will best serve the team in heightening its effectiveness in each of the phases of the Team Spirit Spiral.

The Learning Activities

Spirit Sayings provides thought-provoking perspectives about spirited teams.

Characteristics of Spirited Teams engages participants in describing their own experience of spirited, high-performing teams.

How to Kill Spirit helps the team to become aware of what team members and organizations do to disempower the spirit of individuals and the team.

Walk in Nature: Discovering the Phases of the Spiral involves participants in finding artifacts from nature symbolizing each phase of the Spiral.

The Seasons of a Team's Life: Establishing Team Climate creates understanding of the Team Spirit Spiral, using the changing seasons as a metaphor for the movements of the Spiral.

Discovering the Harmonics That Underlie Spirit creates greater awareness of the values associated with each phase of the Team Spirit Spiral.

Discovering Individual Spirit engages individual team members in considering their own strength of spirit.

Team Spirit Assessment provides data about the team's pattern of consonances and dissonances for each phase of the Spiral.

ACTIVITY

SPIRIT SAYINGS

Learning Goals

1. To promote understanding of various viewpoints about spirit in teams through identification with quotes from notable persons.
2. To foster the development of relationships among team members.

Preparation

1. Create a flip chart display with the heading, Spirit in Team: Important Implications.
2. Photocopy the Perspectives on Spirited Teams and Organizations handout for all participants.

Learning Activity

1. Distribute the Perspectives on Spirited Teams and Organizations handout and ask participants to review the collection of quotes about spirited teams. Have each member choose the quote that most speaks to him or her. Ask that they prepare to explain why they chose that quote. Allow five to eight minutes for reading, choosing and preparing to present quotes.
2. Randomly call on individuals to read and explain their quotes. Record the emerging themes on the flip chart.
3. After listening to all responses, ask the team what occurred for them as a result of this sharing. Work with them to clarify implications for their daily work.

What to Expect

This activity engages participants in considering important perspectives about the spirit operating in teams and organizations expressed in the literature. Participants easily identify with these quotes and like sharing why they made their choices of spirit sayings. They typically connect them with their experience in teams and organizations. After the first volunteer identifies his or her spirit saying, ask how many other team members identified that spirit saying and ask them to explain their reasoning for choosing that specific quote. Considerable energy about spirit in teams and organizations can be created very quickly through this activity.

Approximate time: 30 minutes.

High performance is the swim team that broke all the records, the peace rally that changed the votes, the marching band that blew them away, the proposal team that brought it home, the unit that no one used to believe in, the department that made everyone take notice, the company that always does it better. It is excellence, peak performance, the best, winning, and being on a roll. What's more, it has happened to every one of us some time along the way.

Robert Barthelemy, *High Performance* (1984)

Organizations lack...faith, faith that they can accomplish their purposes in various ways and that they do best when they focus on direction and vision, letting transient forms emerge and disappear. We seem fixated on structures; and we build them strong and complex because they must, we believe, hold back the dark forces that are out to destroy us....The things we fear most in organizations—fluctuations, disturbances, imbalances—need not be signs of an impending disorder that will destroy us. Instead, fluctuations are the primary source of creativity.

Margaret Wheatley, *Leadership and the New Science* (1992)

All...are caught in an inescapable network of mutuality, tied in a single garment of destiny....I can never be what I ought to be until you are what you ought to be, and you can never be what you ought to be until I am what I ought to be. This is the inter-related structure of reality.

Martin Luther King, Jr.

Whatever else high performance and excellence may be based on, they would seem to have something to do with the quality of spirit...human Spirit, our Spirit, the Spirit of our organizations.

Harrison Owen, *Spirit-Transformation and Development in Organizations* (1987)

In many corporations, poverty also exists. It is "spiritual poverty" at its starkest. For large numbers of people, the workplace occupies a majority of their waking hours, and for many, it is the most important place in their lives. It is where they seek meaning and purpose.

Barbara Shipka in Pat Barrentine's *When the Canary Stops Singing—Women's Perspectives on Transforming Business* (1993)

Photocopied from *Building Team Spirit* by Barry Heermann.
Published by McGraw-Hill, ISBN 0-07-028472-5. To order, call 1-800-2MCGRAW.

All the case studies and other research results that have come out
about excellence and peak performance confirm that
both members and observers of excellent organizations consistently feel
the spirit of the organization and the activity,
and that this feeling of spirit is an essential part of the meaning
and value that members and observers place on the activity.

Peter Vaill, *Managing as a Performing Art* (1989)

We at Herman Miller acknowledge
that issues of the heart and spirit matter to each of us... We are emotional
creatures, trying through the vehicles
of product and knowledge and information and relationships
to have an effect for good on one another
both personally and through
what we can do to improve the environment

Max DePree, *Leadership Jazz* (1992)

Our deepest fear is not that we are inadequate.
Our deepest fear is that we are powerful beyond measure.
It is our light, not our darkness, that most frightens us.

Nelson Mandela's 1994 Inaugural Speech

The best test, and the most difficult to administer is:
Do those served grow as persons; do they, while being served,
become healthier, wiser, freer, more autonomous,
more likely themselves to become servants?

Robert Greenleaf, *Servant Leadership* (1977)

The Great Malady of the Twentieth Century,
implicated in all of our troubles
and affecting us individually and socially
is "loss of soul."
When soul is neglected, it doesn't just go away;
it appears symptomatically
in obsessions, addictions, violence, and loss of meaning....
the root problem is that we have lost our wisdom about the soul,
even our interest in it.

Thomas Moore, *Care of the Soul* (1994)

Photocopied from *Building Team Spirit* by Barry Heermann.
Published by McGraw-Hill, ISBN 0-07-028472-5. To order, call 1-800-2MCGRAW.

ACTIVITY

CHARACTERISTICS OF SPIRITED TEAMS

Learning Goals

1. To create the experience of a spirited, high-performing team through the sharing of participants.
2. To distinguish the characteristics of a spirited team, relating these to the Team Spirit Spiral.

Preparation

1. Photocopy the Team Spirit Spiral handout for all participants.
2. Create a flip chart display with the heading, Characteristics of Spirited Teams.
3. Provide notepaper for participants.

Learning Activity

1. Ask participants to identify a time when they participated in a "spirited team," in other words, a team that produced extraordinary results arising out of a unique spirit or energy within the team. Ask that they not limit themselves to their recent work history. Suggest that they look at all of their experience: volunteer work, musical and athletic groups, other work settings, school groups, etc. The defining characteristic of the team is that it was an extraordinary team, a spirited team. Have the participants write notes to themselves clarifying the who, what, where, when, why, and how of the remembered experience. Allow eight minutes for recording their responses.
2. Ask team members to share, in turn, characteristics of their spirited team experience. Record key words on the Characteristics of Spirited Teams flip chart display.

3. In order to prompt the sharing, repeatedly ask the group, What is at the heart of a spirited team? What are the characteristics of extraordinary teams? What is the experience of being a part of such teams? What takes place in the team that produces such impressive results?

4. After all characteristics have been shared and recorded, ask participants to consider the relationship of the ideas they generated to the phases of the Team Spirit Spiral. Distribute the Team Spirit Spiral handout. Emphasize that Team Spirit is merely a useful theory—it is not absolute truth. It is, however, an effective model of what teams need to "do" and "be" in order to achieve high performance. Ask participants to identify the phase of the Spiral for each characteristic, and record the phase in a different color of marker next to the item. Make sure that participants are clear about the relationship of the characteristics they generated to the phases of the Spiral.

5. Explain that one of the purposes of *Building Team Spirit* is to heighten recognition of high performance and spirit, so that participants can be aware of, and even generate, these characteristics in the functioning of their current organizations.

What to Expect

This is a powerful activity because participants share their stories of spirited, high-performing teams, describing, sometimes with great affect, those treasured moments and characteristics of their great team experience. Enthusiasm builds as participants offer their characteristics. It is important that the facilitator mirror the energy and the characteristic identified, carefully using the precise words used by participants, and avoid interpreting or embellishing comments offered by participants. An intellectual understanding of the Team Spirit Spiral begins to develop from these shared experiences and characteristics of spirited teams offered by participants.

Approximate time: 30 minutes.

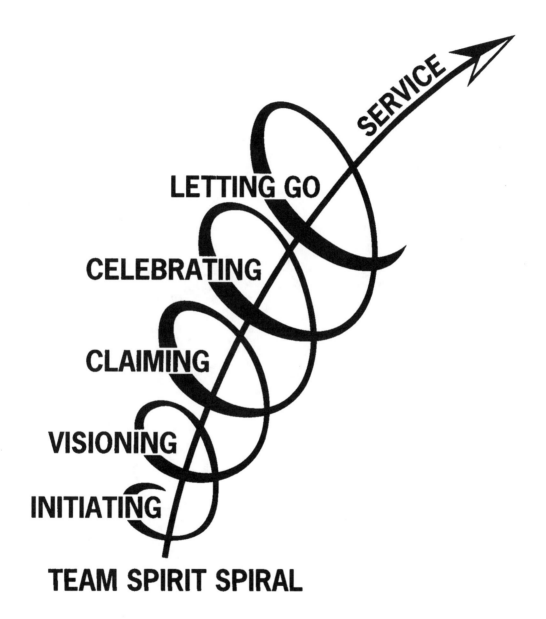

SERVICE

LETTING GO

CELEBRATING

CLAIMING

VISIONING

INITIATING

TEAM SPIRIT SPIRAL

Photocopied from *Building Team Spirit* by Barry Heermann.
Published by McGraw-Hill, ISBN 0-07-028472-5. To order, call 1-800-2MCGRAW.

Learning Goal

To reach agreement about several concrete actions to improve the spirit and performance of the team by first recognizing factors that disempower the spirit of individuals on the team.

Preparation

1. Create three flip chart displays with the headings:

   How to Ensure a Dispirited Team
   Responses to Dispiritedness
   Action Steps

2. Provide notepaper for all participants.

Learning Activity

1. Ask the team what an organization could do to create dispirited teams.
2. As the team identifies what inhibits spirited teams, record their responses on the flip chart display. Upon identifying all of their inhibiting factors, ask the team to identify the two or three most destructive factors that kill off spirit in *this* team. Underline those factors on the flip chart.
3. Request that the team work in pairs to come up with suggestions that would allow the team to respond to the killing factors identified and underscored on the flip chart, recording ideas on the notepaper provided. Provide 10 minutes for work in pairs.

4. Ask the pairs to share their responses. Record their responses on the second flip chart display, and lead the team in a discussion of these responses. Allow 10 to 15 minutes for this discussion.

5. Request that the team identify the next steps they would take to create more spirit in their team. Record those ideas on the third flip chart display.

6. Ask what the team learned about how to respond to dispiritedness.

What to Expect

By discussing dispirited teams, the participants begin to speak of their own, sometimes pent-up, frustrations and concerns. This activity encourages Letting Go. The usefulness of the activity is in the identification of steps to facilitate greater spirit from an understanding of the dispiriting factors existing in the team.

Approximate time: 45-60 minutes.

ACTIVITY
WALK IN NATURE:
DISCOVERING THE PHASES OF THE SPIRAL

Learning Goals

1. To increase awareness and understanding of the phases of the Spiral by engaging the team in a concrete experience that connects meaning to each phase of the Spiral.
2. To foster the development of relationship and connection among team members.

Preparation

1. Arrange for a training site that is adjacent to an outdoor, pastoral, natural setting that team members are permitted to walk into and explore.
2. Prepare a lecturette that clarifies the phases of the Team Spirit Spiral (see Appendix C, lecturette 1).
3. Photocopy the Team Spirit Spiral handout for all participants.

Learning Activity

1. Present a lecturette that clarifies the phases of the Team Spirit Spiral. Distribute the Team Spirit Spiral handout. Briefly explain the consonances and dissonances at each phase.
2. Ask participants to form pairs. Encourage participants to choose an individual they may not normally interact with on a daily basis.
3. Depending on the number of pairs, assign one or two phases of the Spiral to each pair.
4. Direct the pairs to go for a 20-minute walk outside to find objects that symbolize the phase or phases of the Spiral assigned to the pair.

335

5. When the pairs return, have a spokesperson from each pair explain why a particular object was chosen.

6. After the pairs share, ask participants at large to share any insights into the phases of the Spiral gained as a result of this learning activity.

7. If convenient, keep the objects displayed and labeled in the training room, as a reminder of the phases and their meanings. The facilitator can reinforce the phases of the Spiral by referring to those objects during the facilitation of future activities.

What to Expect

This exercise provides a change in scenery, pace, and perspective for the participants to grasp the deeper meaning of the phases of the spiral at a personal and symbolic level. Participants welcome the opportunity to get outdoors and explore nature.

Approximate time: 60 minutes.

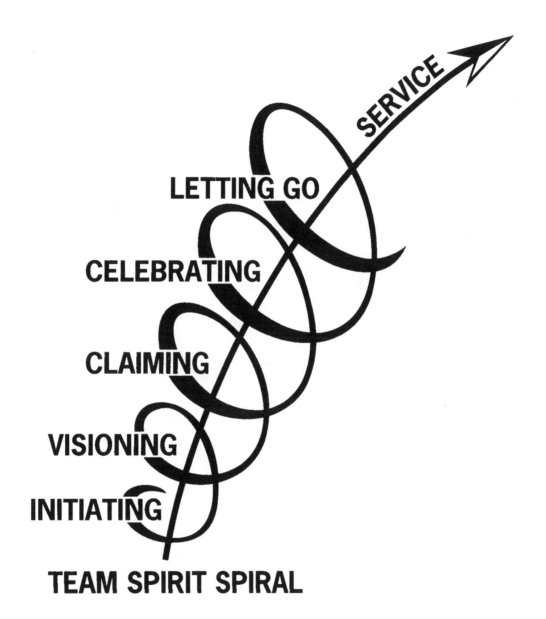

SERVICE

LETTING GO

CELEBRATING

CLAIMING

VISIONING

INITIATING

TEAM SPIRIT SPIRAL

Learning Goals

1. To develop awareness of the phases of the Team Spirit Spiral.
2. To support the team in identifying a team climate that would enhance their spirit as a team and their service to customers by exploring deeper implications of each phase of the Spiral.

(Note: If the goal in the use of this learning activity is to encourage awareness of the phases of the Team Spirit Spiral, end with item four, moving to part seven for closure. Use only learning goal one; preparations one and two; and learning activities one through four. If the goal is to also assist the team in formulating a vision for improving their team climate, use all items in order.)

Preparation

1. Prepare a lecturette that clarifies the phases of the Team Spirit Spiral (see Appendix C, lecturette 1).
2. Photocopy the Team Spirit Spiral handout for all participants.
3. Create four flip chart displays with headings for each of the four seasons of the year.
4. Create five flip chart displays with headings for each of the five phases of the Team Spirit Spiral.
5. Create a flip chart display with the heading, Desired Actions and Behaviors.

Learning Activity

1. Present a lecturette that clarifies the phases of the Team Spirit Spiral. Distribute the Team Spirit Spiral handout. Indicate that the purpose of

this learning activity is to explore deeper implications of the quality of spirit within each phase of the Spiral and to identify the team climate that would best enhance the spirit of this particular team and the service it provides to customers.

2. Note that the movements of the Spiral parallel the movements of nature. Just as in nature there is a natural ebbing and flowing, a constant rising and falling, so it is with the Team Spirit Spiral. The movement of the seasons and the resulting cyclical patterns in nature serve as a useful metaphor.

In spring the soil is prepared, including tilling and plowing and planting of seeds in anticipation of new growth, paralleling the *Initiating* and *Visioning* phases of the Spiral.

In summer the new growth is nurtured through fertilization and maintenance of the crops, paralleling the *Claiming* phase of the Spiral.

In autumn the joyful harvest of the crops parallels the *Celebrating* phase of the Spiral.

In winter the death of vegetation and the land lying dormant parallel the *Letting Go* phase of the Spiral.

3. Explain that in this learning activity the team will explore the qualities associated with each of the seasons of the year and relate the qualities of the seasons to their team. Begin the first part of this learning activity by asking the team to brainstorm the characteristics, tasks, moods, and feelings they associate with each of the four seasons. Record the ideas they generate for each season on the flip charts.

4. After completing the brainstorming on the seasons, focus attention on the Team Spirit Spiral. Briefly review the phases. Point to the ideas generated for each season and ask the team to correlate the phases to the seasons. Circle the words describing the seasons that best fit the team for each phase of the Spiral. After circling all the words members associate with the work of their team, ask what they have observed by participating in this learning activity.

5. For the second part of this learning activity, ask the team to draw upon their brainstorming ideas, choosing words and meanings that they feel drawn to and wish to incorporate in their team process. Ask the team to relate those words and meanings to the Team Spirit Spiral. Begin with Initiating, asking the team to reach consensus on several words that suggest the kind of climate they would like to achieve through Initiating. Do this for each of the phases of the Spiral through Letting Go, recording

their responses on the flip charts. Post the flip chart displays for each phase. Ask the team to reconsider their work and to determine whether these characteristics (aspects of climate) are worth committing themselves to. Reach consensus with the team. Next, request that the team generate the kinds of actions and behaviors that will be required of them to realize those characteristics, recording them on a flip chart. Post the flip chart displays for these desired actions and behaviors.

6. In conclusion, ask if there is a person on the team who would like to be the safeguard for the Initiating characteristics, for the Visioning characteristics, and so on through the Letting Go characteristics. Post those names on the flip chart display identifying the desired characteristics of team climate.

7. Ask participants to share any thoughts or feelings about their work on this learning activity.

What to Expect

This activity encourages metaphorical thinking that fosters creativity and new perspectives. When they consider the seasons of the year, participants are surprised to see how the cycles and images associated with the seasons connect with the phases of the Team Spirit Spiral. The Spiral takes on a more organic and natural feel as a result of this activity. The Visioning work in the second half of the activity continues to build on this metaphor. Images of preparing the soil, sowing the seeds, fertilizing the plants, harvesting the crop, etc., nurture creative thinking about the team's vision.

Approximate time: 60-90 minutes for entire learning activity; 45-60 minutes for abbreviated activity.

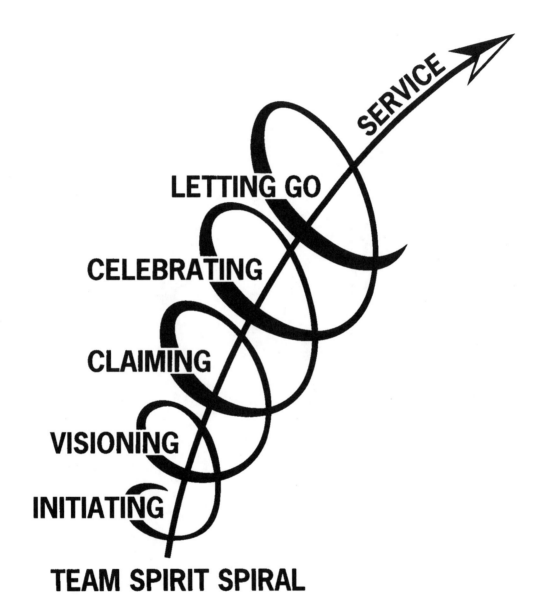

SERVICE

LETTING GO

CELEBRATING

CLAIMING

VISIONING

INITIATING

TEAM SPIRIT SPIRAL

Learning Goals

1. To create greater awareness and understanding of the value structure associated with each phase of the Team Spirit Spiral.
2. To allow team members to work together in subteams to identify how the values (consonances and dissonances) relate to each phase of the Spiral.

Preparation

1. Prepare a lecturette on the team spirit harmonics, that is, the consonances and dissonances teams experience (see Appendix C, lecturette 1).
2. Photocopy the Team Spirit Harmonics handout for all participants.
3. Photocopy the Puzzles handout for all participants.

Learning Activity

1. Present a lecturette on the Team Spirit harmonics, that is, the consonances and dissonances teams experience. Distribute the Team Spirit Harmonics handout. Have participants scan the definitions of consonances and dissonances to ensure understanding. Ask if there are any questions about this system of values expressed as harmonics or about their definitions.
2. Ask the team to form triads. Distribute the Puzzles handout. Clarify that the challenge is to match each consonance or dissonance with a corresponding phase of the Spiral. Ask that all materials related to team spirit, the Spiral, and the harmonics be removed from the tabletops.
3. Pass out the puzzles face down to each team. Tell participants that you will instruct them when to turn their sheets over. Appoint one person from each triad to record the letter symbol representing the appropriate

phase of the Spiral (the right column) in the appropriate space in front of the consonant or dissonant item (the left column). Consonant items are marked with a "c" and dissonant items with a "d." When they have finished matching all harmonics with phases of the Spiral the triad should signal their completion.

4. Ask if there are any questions. When all questions have been answered, signal the triads to begin.

5. Discuss the responses for all parts of the puzzle with the team, achieving consensus on the correct responses.

6. Acknowledge all triads for participating. Ask what the team learned about the relationship of harmonics to the phases of the Team Spirit Spiral.

What to Expect

Participants enjoy this game-like activity. A high level of energy develops during the course of the activity as participants work to generate correct responses to each puzzle. The activity reinforces the value structure that underlies the phases of the Team Spirit Spiral.

Approximate time: 30-45 minutes.

CONSONANCES

(a combination of musical tones that have resolved—that is, they are in agreement)

Service
-*contribution*: generously and freely giving to another
-*aligned execution*: fulfilling, in a unified way, customer and team needs
-*mutual support*: providing reciprocal assistance

Initiating
-*orientation*: becoming familiarized and aware
-*belonging*: feeling allied with and a part of the team
-*trust*: feeling reliant and secure about team members

Visioning
-*shared vision/values*: agreeing on what is possible and its underlying worth and merit
-*compassion*: experiencing empathy and concern for another
-*presence*: deeply experiencing the purpose of the team

Claiming
-*goal/role alignment*: agreeing on the outcome and the means for achieving it
-*organization support*: securing the necessary resources from the organization
-*competence*: developing skills and awareness needed to perform team roles

Celebrating
-*appreciation*: feeling recognized and acknowledged
-*energy*: experiencing vitality and aliveness
-*wonder*: experiencing an unbounded sense of possibility

Letting Go
-*disclosure*: revealing previously suppressed attitudes and opinions
-*constructive feedback*: providing forthright responses that encourage growth
—*completion*: feeling a sense of freedom when everything has been said

DISSONANCES

(a combination of unresolved musical tones)

Service
-*depletion*: feeling used up, unable to freely give to another
-*uncoordinated action*: incompletely fulfilling customer and team needs
-*unsupportiveness*: acting without concern for others

Initiating
-*disorientation*: experiencing disequilibrium and fear
-*alienation*: feeling like a misfit, not a part of the team
-*mistrust*: feeling insecure and cautious about team members

Visioning
-*ambiguous vision/values*: experiencing uncertainty about what is possible—let alone its underlying worth and merit
-*callousness*: being insensitive and harsh
-*aridness*: feeling barren and empty, without a sense of purpose

Claiming
-*nonalignment*: disagreeing about the outcome and means for achieving it
-*nonsupport*: being unable to secure the necessary resources from the organization
-*deficiency*: not having the skills and awareness needed to perform team roles

Celebrating
-*nonappreciation*: not feeling recognized and acknowledged
-*burnout*: feeling used up and ineffective in the team
-*disenchantment*: feeling repelled and put out

Letting Go
-*withheld communication*: concealing attitudes and opinions from others
-*criticism*: offering unsupportive critical feedback
-*incompletion*: feeling regretful about withholding communications

Photocopied from *Building Team Spirit* by Barry Heermann.
Published by McGraw-Hill, ISBN 0-07-028472-5. To order, call 1-800-2MCGRAW.

Puzzle 1

____ 1. withheld communications [d]
____ 2. aridness [d]
____ 3. goal/role alignment [c]
____ 4. orientation [c]
____ 5. aligned execution [c]
____ 6. wonder [c]

a. initiating
b. visioning
c. claiming
d. celebrating
e. letting go
f. service

Puzzle 2

____ 1. unsupportiveness [d]
____ 2. completion [c]
____ 3. mistrust [d]
____ 4. presence [c]
____ 5. competence [c]
____ 6. nonappreciation [d]

a. initiating
b. visioning
c. claiming
d. celebrating
e. letting go
f. service

Puzzle 3

____ 1. organizational support [c]
____ 2. burnout [d]
____ 3. incompletion [d]
____ 4. ambiguous vision/values [d]
____ 5. mutual support [c]
____ 6. belonging [c]

a. initiating
b. visioning
c. claiming
d. celebrating
e. letting go
f. service

Puzzle 4

____ 1. disorientation [d]
____ 2. compassion [c]
____ 3. disclosure [c]
____ 4. appreciation [c]
____ 5. deficiency [d]
____ 6. contribution [c]

a. initiating
b. visioning
c. claiming
d. celebrating
e. letting go
f. service

ACTIVITY
DISCOVERING INDIVIDUAL SPIRIT

Learning Goals

1. To support team members in identifying their individual talents and strengths related to the phases of the Team Spirit Spiral.
2. To engage team members in sharing their strengths.

Preparation

1. Prepare a lecturette on the use of the Team Spirit Spiral for personal development (see Appendix C, lecturette 2).
2. Photocopy the Team Spirit Spiral handout for all participants.
3. Provide notepaper for all participants.

Learning Activity

1. Present a lecturette on the phases of the Team Spirit Spiral as it relates to personal development (see Appendix C, lecturette 2). Distribute the Team Spirit Spiral handout. Ask members of the team to reflect on each phase of the Spiral, and ask them to identify the phase with which they personally have the most comfort. Following the reflection have participants explain why they feel more comfortable with a particular phase (e.g., a team member might respond, "I have the greatest comfort with Visioning because I know I am instinctively innovative and creative in the way I think."). Allow 10 minutes for this sharing.
2. Request that each team member write six to ten personal qualities associated with the phase he or she selected on notepaper (e.g., for Claiming: commitment, single-minded purpose, clarity, accountability, assuredness, and resolution). Allow five minutes.

3. Direct team members to create groups of three in which to share the phase of the Spiral selected and the personal qualities associated with the phase (e.g., "I am best at Claiming. You can count on me following through on what I say I will do. I am fully committed to our work."). Allow four minutes per person.

4. Ask the group to reassemble as a full team. Ask individual team members to briefly share their place on the Spiral. Have them explain the characteristics that exemplify the strength they bring to the phase they chose.

5. After team members have shared their Spiral phases and qualities, ask the group whether they distinguish similarities in the responses. Determine with the group their collective strengths and weaknesses related to the phases of the Spiral. Ask who they could depend on for certain phases of the Spiral and what requests they might like to make of each other as a result of this learning activity.

What to Expect

This activity provides a safe place for participants to share their abilities and capacities in terms of the Team Spirit Spiral. This affirming activity sets the groundwork for the team's work together. It reinforces the Spiral phases, and it causes the team to notice where its strengths lie in relationship to the Spiral.

Approximate time: 45-60 minutes.

Team Spirit Spiral

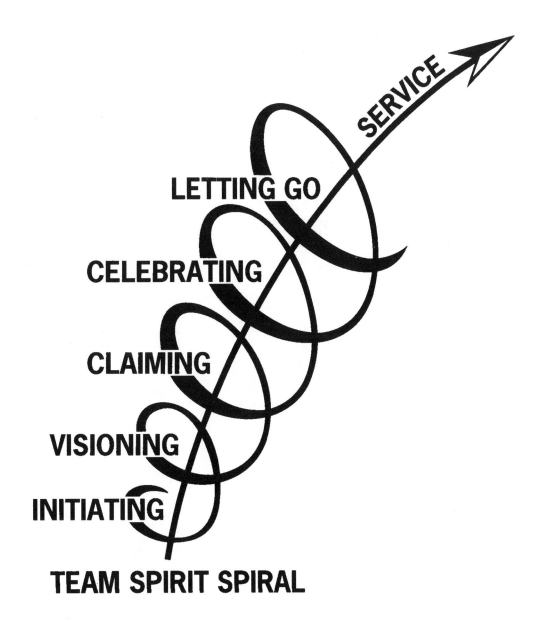

SERVICE

LETTING GO

CELEBRATING

CLAIMING

VISIONING

INITIATING

TEAM SPIRIT SPIRAL

ACTIVITY
TEAM SPIRIT ASSESSMENT

Learning Goals

1. To help the team evaluate its experience working together in relationship to the phases of the Team Spirit Spiral.
2. To provide the team and the facilitator with information to make choices about the experiential learning activities that appear in the remainder of this volume.

Preparation

1. Photocopy the Team Spirit Spiral handout for all participants.
2. Create a flip chart display that duplicates the Team Spirit Assessment form.
3. Photocopy the Team Spirit Assessment handout for all participants.
4. Create a flip chart display with the heading, Action Steps.

Learning Activity

1. Review the phases of the Spiral and the consonances and dissonances in each phase. Distribute the Team Spirit Spiral handout.
2. Distribute the Team Spirit Assessment handout. Direct participants to place a check mark on the scales of the Team Spirit Assessment that indicates where they perceive their team to be for each consonant/dissonant pair in each phase of the Spiral.
3. Record participant responses on the flip chart display of the assessment posted at the front of the room. Ask participants to identify those phases that are most consonant and those phases that are most dissonant. Determine areas of agreement and divergence. Provide feedback to the team on the phases that they perceive as the most consonant and dissonant.

355

4. Generate concrete examples of the most consonant factors. Acknowledge the team for these strengths. Record these consonant factors as "team strengths" on a flip chart.

5. Generate concrete examples of the most dissonant factors. Record these issues on a flip chart as "team weaknesses." After generating several concrete examples of the most significant dissonant factors, ask the team to prioritize them in order of importance.

6. Work with the team to generate action steps that respond to the most critical situations. Record their action steps on the flip chart display.

Note: For a fuller treatment of the Team Spirit Assessment and how to facilitate an in-depth Feedback and Action Planning Session, see Appendix A and the activity in Appendix E, Service: Assessing Team Needs and Choosing Activities for Teams.

What to Expect

This activity is sobering and sometimes a little confrontational for team participants. By responding to the assessment, participants reveal strengths as well as concerns and issues that they hold about their team, e.g., Letting Go issues. Facilitating authenticity and openness on the part of participants is key. The value of this activity is the discussion of concrete examples of both dissonances and consonances that underscore participant assessments. This activity is particularly useful for determining the best combination of activities to meet team needs.

Approximate time: 60 minutes.

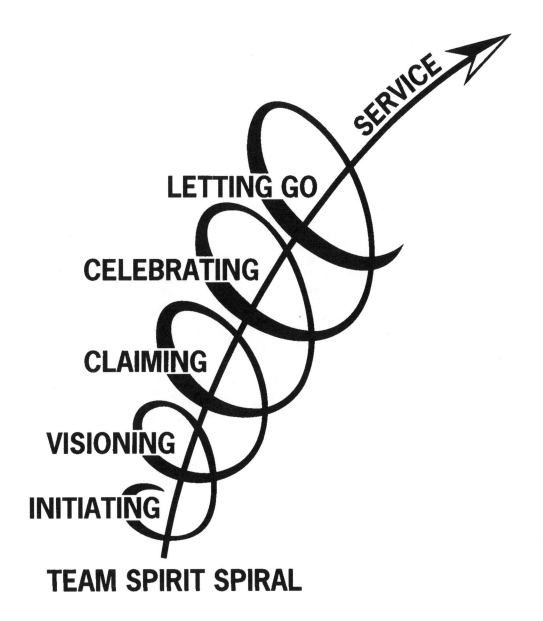

1. Service

contribution |——|——|——|——|——|——|——|——| depletion

aligned execution |——|——|——|——|——|——|——|——| uncoordinated action

mutual support |——|——|——|——|——|——|——|——| unsupportiveness

2. Initiating

orientation |——|——|——|——|——|——|——|——| disorientation

belonging |——|——|——|——|——|——|——|——| alienation

trust |——|——|——|——|——|——|——|——| mistrust

3. Visioning

shared vision/values |——|——|——|——|——|——|——|——| ambiguous vision/values

compassion |——|——|——|——|——|——|——|——| callousness

presence |——|——|——|——|——|——|——|——| aridness

4. Claiming

goal/role alignment |——|——|——|——|——|——|——|——| nonalignment

organization support |——|——|——|——|——|——|——|——| nonsupport

competence |——|——|——|——|——|——|——|——| deficiency

5. Celebrating

appreciation |——|——|——|——|——|——|——|——| nonappreciation

energy |——|——|——|——|——|——|——|——| burnout

wonder |——|——|——|——|——|——|——|——| disenchantment

6. Letting Go

disclosure |——|——|——|——|——|——|——|——| withheld communication

constructive |——|——|——|——|——|——|——|——| criticism

feedback completion |——|——|——|——|——|——|——|——| incompletion

E

The Spirit of the Facilitator

The best test, and the most difficult to administer is:
Do those served grow as persons;
do they, while being served, become healthier, wiser, freer,
more autonomous, more likely themselves to become servants?
Robert Greenleaf

The critical work of connecting to the *spirit* of the team arises out of the *facilitation* of team spirit. Like the shaman in native cultures, the facilitator fills the role of moving the group to the discovery of its spirit. The facilitator works with teams to discover their essence. It is the facilitator who breathes life into the idea of spirit in teams and...

creates the awareness,

fosters skills and abilities,

serves as the catalyst for the development of team values, and

models team spirit.

At the core of the facilitation of team spirit is the Service provided to create the necessary awareness, skills, and values for each team member who participates.

As suggested in the Introduction, there are two broad categories of facilitators of team spirit. There will be facilitators who use *Building Team Spirit* like a cookbook, selecting recipes on a periodic basis that respond to particular needs of the team. There will be other facilitators who will:

- commit to using team spirit in a comprehensive, in-depth way,
- draw upon the model and the tenets of spirit in teams presented in Chapters 1 and 2, and
- systematically draw upon the team spirit learning activities in this volume for the teams that they serve.

It is for this latter category of facilitator that this appendix material is intended.

Choosing to facilitate team spirit learning activities in this comprehensive way is different from choosing to facilitate other training and development activities. This choice is not merely about the delivery of a collection of activities that address Team Spirit in teams. It is also about a potentially deeper, more challenging, and rewarding journey.

The choice to be a facilitator of team spirit learning activities in this way can be a commitment to one's inner work and development in each of the phases of the Spiral. It means taking on an inner journey that manifests itself in being present and committed to teams engaged in team spirit. It means the facilitators know their own issues and actively embrace them. It means *being* team spirit not only at the front of the room but in life.

We urge facilitators, committed to this deeper relationship to team spirit, to reflect, dwell on, and access each phase of the Team Spirit Spiral, experiencing their work with team spirit at both intrapersonal and interpersonal levels, distinct from the team level that is the focus of their facilitation role. The rationale is that facilitators who do not practice, say, Claiming or Celebrating in their lives and work, will have more difficulty *being* who they need to be to facilitate effective Claiming or Celebrating in teams.

Excellent team spirit facilitation occurs out of...

generating excitement, acceptance, and expectation for participation (*Initiating*)

creating relationship (*Initiating*)

supporting the team to create belonging, trust, and orientation within the team (*Initiating*)

creating possibility for the team to come to grips with its own harmonics (*Visioning*)

extracting the "gem" from the insights of participants (*Visioning*)

extrapolating and moving the "gem" to a deeper level of relevance for the team (*Visioning*)

being present to the unique spirit of the team (*Visioning*)

supporting the team in its efforts to reveal its own destiny and soul (*Visioning*)

mastering the materials, components, modules, and resources of team spirit (*Claiming*)

handling all of the physical requirements necessary to deliver team spirit programs (*Claiming*)

affirming team members' capacity to claim the use of team spirit in the team (*Claiming*)

claiming one's capacity to facilitate and lead team spirit sessions (*Claiming*)

acknowledging participants for their contributions (*Celebrating*)

acknowledging participants for their courage and their commitment to the team (*Celebrating*)

celebrating the uniqueness and differences of team members (*Celebrating*)

supporting the team in embracing and working through its dissonances (*Letting Go*)

providing constructive feedback and encouraging participants to do likewise (*Letting Go*)

disclosing what is true and encouraging participants to do likewise (*Letting Go*)

developing the capacity of the team to work with the dark side (*Letting Go*)

demonstrating undefended receptivity—the capacity to listen to team dissonances (*Letting Go*)

helping the team connect to its spirit (*Service*)

facilitating awareness, skills, and values that support spirited teams (*Service*)

moving team members to where they "connect" at a deep level regarding their work (*Service*)

keeping one's awareness outside oneself and on the commitment to the team (*Service*)

returning the team to its own unique harmonics (*Service*)

trusting the group to discover its spirit and make whatever improvements are necessary (*Service*)

creating awareness that the "breath breathes the team"—i.e., supporting the team in discovering its own inner wisdom and capacity to serve customers (*Service*)

Note: These considerations can be used by a facilitator to reflect on his or her effectiveness in facilitating team spirit sessions, and cofacilitators can debrief each other after offering a team spirit activity or a series of activities using these considerations.

Achieving greater facility in delivering team spirit learning activities may lead some facilitators to an interest in furthering their personal and professional growth. These facilitators may benefit from organization development training offered by the NTL Institute, such as the Human Interaction Laboratory or Group Process Consulting, as well as personal development programs such as the Forum, offered by Landmark Education, among existing programs offered for personal and organizational development.

The learning activities in this appendix are designed to support the facilitator in the development of these awarenesses and competencies. However, the commitment to developing team spirit in one's own life involves more than engaging in a set of activities. It requires an ongoing commitment to the growth and development of one's own spirit and thoughtful attention to each of the phases of the Spiral.

The learning activities in this appendix can be used by a single facilitator or by cofacilitators. The first seven activities support facilitators in discerning the deeper implications of spirit in all aspects of their lives, especially their roles as facilitators, and the last activity provides instruction and coaching on assessing team needs and planning the composition of team spirit learning activities.

The Learning Activities

Embracing and Coaching Facilitator Dissonance helps facilitators to discover those phases of the Team Spirit Spiral that are core considerations in their lives, developing a coaching relationship for embracing those phases.

Initiating: Developing a Powerful Cofacilitator Relationship assists facilitators in developing an effective cofacilitation relationship by discussing what each facilitator needs and by pledging particular support to each other.

Visioning the Potential of the Team: Dialogue with a Wisdom Figure provides facilitators with a process for Visioning the kind of impact they wish to have with a team that they are supporting.

Claiming: Briefing and Debriefing with Your Cofacilitator helps cofacilitators to create alignment and purpose at the outset of a team spirit learning activity and to acknowledge accomplishments and provide feedback at the completion of the facilitation.

Celebrating: Stories of Effective Team Facilitation provides a context for a team of facilitators to tell stories of effective team spirit facilitation and to design enhanced approaches to the delivery of team spirit that builds upon the success stories.

Letting Go: Completion Exercise provides an opportunity for a team of facilitators to formally let go of incompletions related to their facilitation.

Serving As a Team Spirit Facilitator: Choosing a Symbol engages facilitators in exploring the meaning of Service as facilitators of team spirit learning activities, identifying Service with a symbol.

Service: Assessing Team Spirit Needs and Choosing Activities for Teams helps facilitators to gather data regarding the needs of teams and to choose appropriate learning activities.

Learning Goals

1. To discover that phase of the Team Spirit Spiral that is most closely linked to your effectiveness as a facilitator.
2. To develop a coaching relationship for embracing a critical phase of the Team Spirit Spiral related to your growth personally, professionally, and as a facilitator.

Preparation

1. Provide notepaper.
2. Arrange a meeting space for meetings with a coaching partner.

Learning Activity for Facilitator

1. Effectiveness as a facilitator requires attention to and discernment of your own process, and reflection on the Team Spirit Spiral. The Team Spirit Spiral is not only a way to understand the spirit of teams. It is also a useful way to consider the dynamics of whole organizations, interpersonal relationships, and personal development. Consider the operational levels of the Team Spirit Spiral.
2. Reflect on the phases of the Team Spirit Spiral in your own life in terms of your relationships with family, colleagues, and friends as well as your current life and work challenges.
3. As you reflect on the Spiral, identify the phase where you feel the most comfort and personal mastery (consonance) and the least comfort and mastery (dissonance). For most persons there is a pattern that cuts across all dimensions of living, whether family, avocation, or vocation.

367

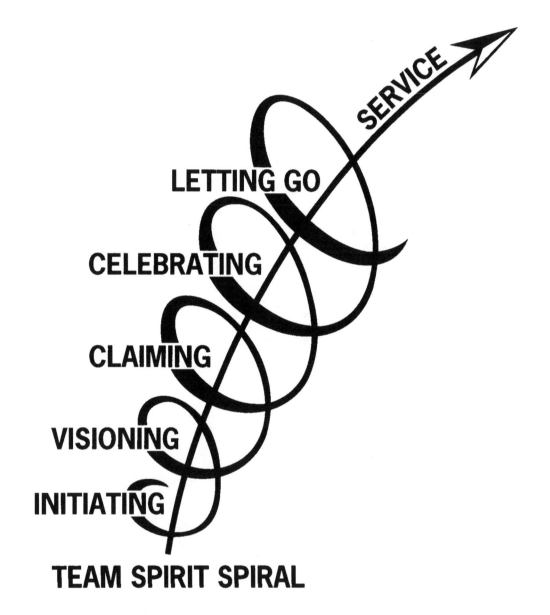

On notepaper explain why you feel most comfortable and personally masterful with the phase you selected. Similarly, identify the phase in which you feel the least successful and that needs the most developing at this time in your life, and explain why you feel less successful.

4. Identify someone who is willing to coach you regarding this phase of your Spiral. You may wish to establish a coaching relationship with your cofacilitator or a valued colleague or friend. Share with this person how both the consonant phase and the dissonant phase manifest themselves in your daily life. Provide specific, concrete examples for all aspects of your life, particularly in your role as a facilitator. Disclose issues to your coaching partner that are related to your dissonant phase and how you feel inhibited in moving from dissonance to consonance. Ask for feedback and assistance from your coach.

5. If your coach is your cofacilitator, request ongoing feedback on how your work on that phase is affecting your facilitation during team spirit activities that you facilitate together

6. Develop a regular meeting schedule for check-ins with your coaching partner.

What to Expect

It is important for facilitators to take on awareness of the intrapersonal dimension of their own development related to team spirit. The Spiral is operating within the facilitator as well as the teams and team members that benefit from team spirit training. This activity is designed to assist the facilitator in clarifying his or her unique pattern of consonance and dissonance in personal and work realms, and especially as a facilitator. Taking on one's own development is best supported in a coaching relationship.

Approximate time: 30 minutes (plus 30 minutes for each coaching session).

Learning Goals

1. To develop an effective cofacilitation relationship by discussing what each facilitator needs in the relationship to ensure effectiveness.
2. To pledge support to each other.

Preparation

1. Arrange a meeting space for cofacilitators to communicate their needs, prior to delivering their first team spirit activity.
2. Provide notepaper.

Learning Activity for Facilitators

1. Cofacilitators should take time to explore their interests and passions in life and work, revealing their respective orientations about facilitation. Each facilitator should tell his or her story, exploring commonalties and points of connection.
2. Out of this conversation both facilitators should consider what they need from the other to optimize their work in facilitating team spirit activities. It is imperative that facilitators model the Team Spirit Spiral, disclosing what is important to them, making requests of each other in the clearest possible terms, and recording those requests on the notepaper provided.
3. After making all requests, the facilitators should indicate what they are willing to provide, exploring how they can mutually support each other in all aspects of their facilitation of team spirit activities.

What to Expect

In this activity facilitators are afforded the opportunity to ask for what they need. They are empowered by making such requests of each other. This activity provides the opportunity to design specific means for supporting each other in all aspects of their facilitation together.

Approximate time: 60-90 minutes.

Learning Goals

1. To vision the kind of impact facilitators wish to have on a team that requests team spirit training.
2. To identify what facilitators need to do and who facilitators need to be to best deliver team spirit training.

Preparation

Provide notepaper.

Learning Activity for Facilitators

1. Effectiveness in facilitating team spirit training occurs best when facilitators have developed a vibrant vision for the process and outcome of the team. Facilitators who focus and are clear about what they intend to have happen are more vital and resourceful.
2. Begin this activity by releasing the tensions of the day: Relax, breathe deeply, and listen to your inner voice. From this place of quiet consider all of those persons in your life who have served as sources of wisdom and inspiration to you. When ready, make a list of these wisdom figures on the notepaper provided.
3. From this list select one person with whom you will dialogue about the team you will be facilitating.
4. In preparation for the dialogue, draw a vertical line down the middle of a page of notepaper, creating two columns: one for your queries and one for your wisdom figure's responses. Select from the following questions or develop other questions that you wish to pose to your wisdom figure.

- What would a breakthrough for this team look like?
- What will I need to do and who will I need to be to facilitate such a breakthrough?
- What do you perceive to be the greatest inner strength that I can draw upon in facilitating team spirit with this team?
- What general coaching do you have for me?

5. When finished with the dialogue, make notes to which you can refer that will remind you of the vision you have for the team you are working with, clarify who you will need to be, and identify what you will need to do to accomplish that result.

What to Expect

This activity supports facilitators in exploring their vision for the process and outcome for the team they will work with, as well as who they will need to be and what they will need to do to accomplish that result. It is useful to complete this activity before beginning work with any new team or with an ongoing team relationship that involves facilitation challenges.

Approximate time: 60-90 minutes.

Learning Goals

1. To create energy, wonder, alignment, and purpose between cofacilitators at the outset of a team spirit learning activity.
2. To acknowledge accomplishments, disclose concerns, and provide constructive feedback at the completion of a team spirit learning activity.

Preparation

Arrange a meeting space for communicating before the beginning of a team spirit learning activity and at the completion of the activity.

Learning Activity for Facilitators

1. Cofacilitators meet to create energy, wonder, alignment, and purpose at the outset of a team spirit activity. During this session the facilitators separately assert their commitment to the team and clarify their visions of the session they will facilitate, identifying a particular phase of the Team Spirit Spiral that they intend to model during the learning activity (e.g., one facilitator might model Celebrating consciously, acknowledging participant contributions and creating a celebratory mood within the team; the other facilitator might model Claiming, being mindful of all of the facilitation guidelines and parameters of the activity).
2. During this briefing session the cofacilitators make requests of each other and review the guidelines and ground rules for the activity and how they will share their cofacilitation of the activity.
3. Immediately after the completion of the team spirit learning activity, the cofacilitators meet to complete their work together. During this session the cofacilitators acknowledge their accomplishments and what worked best about their facilitation of the activity. They also disclose any con-

cerns they might have about their work together, providing constructive feedback about how this activity might be enhanced in the future and how they might best go about cofacilitating their next team spirit learning activity based upon this experience.

4. When final evaluation data are accumulated about the team spirit workshop, the cofacilitators meet again to review the evaluations and plan their next team spirit learning activity.

What to Expect

This activity allows cofacilitators to align their work in delivering team spirit activities. At the completion of facilitating team spirit with a team, this activity provides a structure for cofacilitators to complete their work together, using the learning from this experience to plan their next facilitation of team spirit.

Approximate time: 30 minutes (briefing); 30 minutes (debriefing).

Learning Goals

1. To provide a context for facilitators to tell stories of effective team spirit facilitation.
2. To design enhanced approaches for the delivery of team spirit activities that build upon the successful stories shared by the facilitators.

Preparation

1. Provide notepaper.
2. Create two flip chart displays with the headings, Threads and Action Ideas.

Learning Activity for Facilitators

Note: This activity is designed to be used in organizations in which several colleagues, three or more, serve as facilitators of team spirit and have a breadth of experience using team spirit learning activities. With slight modification the activity can work as a wrap-up for cofacilitators who have tailored a systematic application of team spirit activities to the needs of a particular team.

1. Participating facilitators describe, on the notepaper provided, a time when they were particularly effective in delivering team spirit activities, telling the stories of their effective applications, using the journalistic Who, What, Where, When, Why, and How framework. Allow 15 minutes for reflection and writing.
2. When all facilitators have finished, they individually tell their stories. As the stories are told, the facilitators should listen for patterns, seeking consensus about an underlying thread or threads that run through their

stories of success. Record the threads or themes on the first flip chart display.

3. The facilitators engage in an inquiry about what is at the heart of effective team spirit facilitation.

4. The facilitators explore ways in which they might reinforce and extend their effectiveness in the delivery of team spirit activities. Record these action ideas on the second flip chart display.

What to Expect

This activity generates considerable energy and a celebratory mood among facilitators. The key to this activity is in transitioning from telling the stories of spirited team spirit facilitation in the past to discovering enhanced means for facilitating team spirit in future work.

Approximate time: 60-90 minutes.

LETTING GO: COMPLETION EXERCISE

Learning Goals

1. To provide the opportunity for facilitators to let go of incompletions related to their facilitation of team spirit activities.
2. To identify action steps for responding to the situations and issues addressed in this activity.

Preparation

1. Provide notepaper.
2. Create two flip chart displays with the headings, Letting Go Issues/Concerns and Action Ideas.

Note: Like the previous activity, this Letting Go activity is designed for use in organizations in which several colleagues, three or more, serve as facilitators of team spirit and have a breadth of experience using team spirit learning activities. With slight modification the activity can work as a wrap-up for cofacilitators who have tailored a systematic application of team spirit activities to the needs of a particular team.

Learning Activity for Facilitators

1. The facilitators identify on notepaper those persons, situations, facilitation approaches, issues, etc., that they would like to let go of.
2. When all facilitators have finished, they individually describe the dissonance they felt in delivering team spirit sessions. These Letting Go issues, situations, etc., are recorded on the first flip chart display.
3. The facilitators engage in a discussion about what they might do individually and as cofacilitators to avoid these dissonances, including action

379

ideas describing how they might modify given activities to enhance their effectiveness. Action ideas are recorded on the second flip chart display.

What to Expect

Facilitators experience a release as a result of Letting Go of those persons, situations, issues, etc., that have been disturbing for them. Development and implementation of action ideas enables facilitators to continuously improve their effectiveness with teams.

Approximate time: 60-120 minutes.

ACTIVITY
SERVING AS A TEAM SPIRIT FACILITATOR:
CHOOSING A SYMBOL

Learning Goal

To explore the meaning of Service as a facilitator of team spirit by identifying a symbol that personalizes the individual beliefs, values, and meaning placed on Service.

Preparation

1. Locate an outdoor, pastoral, natural setting for taking a walk.
2. Have notepaper or a journal available.

Learning Activity for Facilitators

1. Begin by reflecting on Service as a facilitator, and what it means to serve teams using team spirit. On notepaper or in a journal, record thoughts that come to mind about Service and being a servant to teams.
2. Take a walk outdoors and look for an object in the natural environment that symbolizes the essence of Service for you.
3. After locating a symbol of service, quietly concentrate on your object, considering what the symbol teaches you about your role as a facilitator. Record your reflections on notepaper or in a journal.
4. When facilitating the Symbolizing Service activity described in Chapter 8, be sure to bring your symbol with you to the session so that you can share it with the team.

What to Expect

This activity supports facilitators in deepening their awareness of Service and their commitment to serve teams.

Approximate time: 30-60 minutes.

Learning Goals

1. To identify team spirit dynamics and needs of teams.
2. To choose and sequence team spirit learning activities for the team.

Preparation

1. Locate the Team Spirit Assessment activity in Appendix D.
2. Locate Guidelines for Using the Team Spirit Assessment and Facilitating the Feedback and Action Planning Session in Appendix A.
3. Locate Guidelines for Conducting Effective Team Interviews in Appendix B

Learning Activity for Facilitators

The first step in facilitating team spirit activities with teams is to gather data regarding the team's pattern of consonance and dissonance and predominant phase or phases in the Team Spirit Spiral. Three resources are provided to assist you in gathering this data:

- The Team Spirit Assessment activity in Appendix D
- Guidelines for Using the Team Spirit Assessment and Facilitating the Feedback and Action Planning Session in Appendix A
- Guidelines for Conducting Effective Team Interviews in Appendix B

The Team Spirit Assessment activity is a two-hour experience that allows a team to reflect on its work in terms of the Team Spirit Spiral and the underlying harmonics and to identify actions it can take to move one or two key dissonances to consonances.

383

The Appendix A material, Guidelines for Using the Team Spirit Assessment and Facilitating the Feedback and Action Planning Session, describes an in-depth, one-day assessment process. This process incorporates the Team Spirit Assessment in a modified form and provides for a thorough exploration of dissonances and consonances in a feedback session. It culminates with an action planning phase that provides blueprints for the team to enhance team spirit and performance.

The Guidelines for Conducting Effective Team Interviews that appear in Appendix B provide the means for gathering data from a sample of team members through interviews. This data is then fed back to the team at a later time.

There are various ways of collecting and processing data about the team all of which can guide you in the selection and sequencing of team spirit activities.

1. The first option, the two-hour assessment activity, should only be used after the team has mastered and is conversant with team spirit principles. One or more activities from the context-building material in Appendix D or selected use of Initiating activities would serve as a useful prelude to this assessment option. This activity is not effective with start-up teams as they do not have sufficient experience to use the assessment meaningfully. Mature teams get the most value from this activity. From the two-hour assessment you will have sufficient information to choose activities that support the specific needs of the team.

2. The second option, the full-day feedback and action planning process, is suggested for later use with the team. It is critical that the team have a sufficient base of experience working together to respond to the assessment meaningfully. It is advisable to have completed substantial work with team spirit so that team members are grounded not only in team spirit principles but also team spirit skills and values.

3. The third option, interviews of representative team members, is appropriate to determine team spirit activities for mature teams that you are working with for the first time.

When designing your use of team spirit activities, keep in mind that you may wish to combine activities or modify them with structures that you may have used in other team trainings. The key to the effective use of team spirit activities is to refocus participants on deeper issues related to their work and to the spirit that influences their effectiveness. For a road map of possible applications of team spirit activities, see the Introduction.

What to Expect

This activity provides important data about the phases of development and the needs of client teams. From this data, facilitators can tailor the learning activities in this book to the needs of the team. Use of the in-depth feedback and action planning component requires sensitive and thoughtful facilitation. As suggested previously, facilitators anticipating extensive facilitation of feedback and action planning will benefit from organization development training offered by the NTL Institute, such as the Human Interaction Laboratory or Group Process Consulting, as well as personal development programs such as the Forum, offered by Landmark Education.

Bibliography

Autry, J. *Love and Profit—The Art of Caring Leadership.* New York: Avon Books, 1991.

Barrentine, P., Ed. *When the Canary Stops Singing—Women's Perspectives on Transforming Business.* San Francisco: Berrett-Koehler, Inc., 1993.

Block, P. *Stewardship.* San Francisco: Berrett-Koehler, Inc., 1993.

Bolman, L. G., and Deal, T. E. *Leading with Soul—An Uncommon Journey of Spirit.* San Francisco: Jossey-Bass Publishers, 1995.

Chappell, Tom. *The Soul of a Business—Managing for Profit and the Common Good.* New York: Bantam Books, 1993.

Conger, J., and associates. *Spirit at Work—Discovering the Spirituality in Leadership.* San Francisco: Jossey-Bass Publishers, 1994.

Csikszentmihalyi, M. *Flow—The Psychology of Optimal Experience.* New York: HarperCollins Publishers, 1990.

Drexler, A., Sibbet, D., and Forrester, R. *The Team Performance Model—Blueprints for Productivity and Satisfaction.* Bethel, Maine: National Training Labs, 1988.

Fox, M. *Creation Spirituality.* San Francisco: Harper and Row, 1991.

Fox, M. *Original Blessing.* Santa Fe: Bear & Co., 1983.

Fox, M. *The Reinvention of Work.* San Francisco: Harper and Row, 1993.

Gibb, J. *Trust: A New View of Personal and Organizational Development.* Los Angeles: The Guild of Tutors Press, 1978.

Greenleaf, R. *Servant Leadership—A Journey into the Nature of Legitimate Power and Greatness.* New York: Paulist Press, 1977.

Heermann, B. "Spirit in Team." In Renesch, J., and DeFoore, B., Eds., *The New Bottom Line: Bringing Heart and Soul to Business.* San Francisco: New Leaders Press/Sterling and Stone, 1996.

387

Jantsch, E. *The Self-Organizing Universe*. Elmsford, N.Y.: Pergamon Press, 1980.

Jaworski, J. *Synchronicity: The Inner Path of Leadership*. San Francisco: Berrett-Koehler, Inc., 1996.

Jones, L. *Jesus CEO—Using Ancient Wisdom for Visionary Leadership*. New York: Hyperion, 1995.

Kolb, D. *Experiential Learning: Experience As the source of Learning and Development*. Englewood Cliffs, N. J.: Prentice Hall, 1984.

Kriegel, R., and Kriegel, M.H. *The C Zone: Peak Performance under Pressure*. New York: Doubleday, 1984.

Owen, H. *Spirit-Transformation and Development in Organizations*. Potomac, Md: Abbott Publishing, 1987.

Renesch, J., Ed. *New Traditions in Business—Spirit and Leadership in the 21st Century*. San Francisco: Berrett-Koehler, Inc., 1992.

Renesch, J., and DeFoore, B., Eds. *Rediscovering the Soul of Business: A Renaissance of Values*. San Francisco: New Leaders Press/Sterling and Stone, 1995.

Renesch, J., and DeFoore, B., Eds. *The New Bottom Line: Bringing Heart and Soul to Business*. San Francisco: New Leaders Press/Sterling and Stone, 1996.

Richards, D. *Artful Work—Awakening Joy, Meaning, and Commitment in the Workplace*. San Francisco: Berrett-Koehler, Inc., 1995.

Spears, L., Ed. *Reflections on Leadership—How Robert Greenleaf's Theory of Servant Leadership Influenced Today's Top Management Thinkers*. New York: John Wiley & Sons, Inc., 1995.

Vaill, P. *Learning As a Way of Being*. San Francisco: Jossey-Bass, 1996.

Vaill, P. *Managing As a Performing Art*. San Francisco: Jossey-Bass, 1989.

Wheatley, M. J. *Leadership and the New Science—Learning about Organizations from an Orderly Universe*. San Francisco: Berrett-Koehler, Inc., 1992.

Wheatley, M. J., and Kellner-Rogers, M. *A Simpler Way*. San Francisco: Berrett-Koehler, Inc., 1996.

Whitehead, Albert North. *The Aims of Education and Other Essays*. New York: Free Press, 1967.

Index

TOPICS

NAMES

ABOUT THE TEAM SPIRIT PROGRAM

The learning activities in *Building Team Spirit* grew out of the experience of the Expanded Learning Institute in providing a comprehensive process for organization and team development called Team Spirit. The Team Spirit Program is based on research on high-performing teams and organizations and is designed to create new spirit in the workplace. It does this by engaging a team in a probing exploration of its identity, values, and purpose. Team Spirit is currently used in numerous Fortune 500 companies as well as major not-for-profit agencies. Team Spirit consists of a series of workshops and interventions that nurture spirited, high-performing teams, including a 60-item diagnostic assessment that provides reliable data on the spirit of the team, allowing teams to plan actions tailored to their own needs.

Access to the comprehensive Team Spirit Program is provided through the four-day Team Spirit Certification course. This course prepares individuals to serve as Team Spirit Facilitator/Consultants in their organization or in organizations that they consult with. The course leads to a license agreement that gives the Facilitator/Consultant maximum flexibility to deliver Team Spirit programs without royalty or license fees. There are currently about 200 certified Team Spirit Facilitator/Consultants.

For information about Team Spirit or the Certification, or to receive the Team Spirit Newsletter, please call the Expanded Learning Institute at 800-340-8385 or e-mail to: SPIRIT_AT_WORK@coax.net. You can also reach us through our website page: @http//www.coax.net/SPIRIT_AT_WORK. The Expanded Learning Institute is based in Yellow Springs, Ohio and Delmar, California. Barry Heermann is the President and founder.

ABOUT THE AUTHOR

Barry Heermann, Ph.D. is the Executive Director of the Expanded Learning Institute in Dayton, Ohio. Barry is an organizational consultant and a core faculty member of the Graduate School of the Union Institute. He has served as a faculty member, department head, dean, and vice president in public and private institutions, and he is the author of two books and three New Directions' editions published by Jossey-Bass on adult and experiential learning themes. Barry's reflection on team development, "Spirit in Team," appears in the book, *The New Bottom Line: Bringing Heart and Soul to Business*, (New Leaders Press/Sterling and Stone, 1996).